When Kingdoms Collide
A battle with spirits in Africa

When Kingdoms Collide
A battle with spirits in Africa

P. Frederick

Copyright © 2019, 2021 Patricia Frederick

All rights reserved. No part of this publication may be reproduced or transmitted in any form or by any means without the prior written permission of the author or publisher. For permission requests, write to the publisher, addressed "Attention: Permissions Coordinator," at the address below.

ISBN: 978-1-7336956-7-1

All scripture quotations, unless otherwise indicated, are taken from the Holy Bible, New International Version®, NIV®. Copyright © 1973, 1978, 1984, 2011 by Biblica, Inc.™ Used by permission. All rights reserved worldwide.
Scripture quotations marked (NKJV) are taken from the New King James Version®. Copyright © 1982 by Thomas Nelson. Used by permission. All rights reserved.

First printing edition 2019

Cover image from Adobe Stock
Cover layout and design by M. Gysbers

For more information, contact: P O Box 270413, St Louis MO 63127

This book is dedicated to:

My sweet friend and spiritual sister Annette, your heart and your sweet spirit are so rare, it's beyond precious.

Merlin, for standing by my side no matter what comes against us. You're a man of honor and integrity that I will always stand behind.

And to my Lord and Savior. Abba [Father], to you be all the praise and glory, for without you, I would not want to exist. I praise you forever and ever, my Lord.

Contents

Foreword
Introduction...1
And so it begins..5
God's Hidden Preparation...6
God is Setting Up the Launch......................................10
God's Hand...13
Warnings Begin..16
The Mine Field 20
Combat Begins...21
Boundaries Drawn..23
The Mission Begins...26
Vision Fulfilled..29
Adjusting to the Atmosphere.......................................31
Stay Awake..42
The Convergence...45
Exercise in Humility and Humor.................................49
On the "Lighter" Side..53
The Creep of Religiosity..56
Simple but Not Easy..63
It Becomes Personal..72
Americanized Thinking..83
Choosing "The Way" vs. Living by "The Rules"........85
Ignition Point...93
Axe Man Standoff..105
Keep it Moving..111
We are doing what?!..114
Find "The One"..123
We Were Being Followed..132

The Manipulation Begins	136
Church Unchained	139
Friendly Fire	157
Strength Under Siege	160
The Battle Before the War	163
The Battle Rages On	172
"Enough!"	179
The Plot Thickens	181
Vindication Begins	187
Demons Doubling Down	194
Really?!	197
The Festival	211
Day 1	217
Spirit of Suicide Expelled	238
Flashbacks	244
The Shift	248
I Told You So	250
Infestation	265
Warning or Preparation	276
Holy Ground	278
The Next Level	283
The Final Battle	293
Supercharged	298
Still Not Done	304
The Next Level – The Takeaway	308
Conclusion	323

Foreword

There are not many people in my life who have made the kind of impact as Patricia Frederick. Patricia, whom I call Trish, and I met on a Sunday morning at the church we were attending. Over a few months, I noticed her often moving around the sanctuary during worship time, talking to and praying for people, but we had never spoken. It was a short interaction after we introduced ourselves that morning, but she looked into my eyes and told me, "I would take a bullet for you." The best comeback I could muster was, "I'm not sure how to process that." How can she be serious? We just met a few moments ago! This was not casual banter, but an example of Trish speaking out what God instructed her to say. That may have been normal for her, but it took quite a while for me to understand this way of hearing from God and then the consequential struggle obedience. Over the next years, we learned to share with each other revelations as they come in, helping each other interpret and determine the instructions to act. Now we minister side-by-side in a number of ways, recognizing how God designed our partnership to be much stronger than doubling the number. Together, our gifts mesh in a way that reach people in ways we could not have predicted. There are stories in When Kingdoms Collide that will elaborate.

During that season of my life, I was discovering the hard way of how to allow God to have His way with me. Small step by small step I started doing things that, in my way of thinking, I had no qualifications for. I nervously began responding to the Spirit's urges. Little things like praying for people without knowing them; letting go of my need to be in control by having me stop for someone on the street and give them a snack and message from Papa; and learning how to see people in the Spirit and then simply love from God's perspective. It was radical change, no longer the master of my plans and acting only on His. I believe this is the main root of ministry.

Trish has proven herself to be a fiercely loyal woman of God, to her family, myself, and others close to her. Her heart is designed to give, sharing herself in various ministry pathways. To those paralyzed by a life crisis, struggling with various types of oppression, and anyone who has reached a point where they desire change in their lives. Time after time, I've seen Trish drop important things and go. The fruit of her ministry is evident, as long as God directs her steps, radical breakthroughs will come to those who truly seek. Trish operates from love, but some experience a raw bluntness that reveals a sense of urgency God has dropped on her. She has no time to waste with empty flowery words when God is urging us to get right with Him and stop being our own worst enemy.

Perhaps what Trish is most known for is a level of spiritual gifting that goes beyond what is seen in cultural Christian circles. The authenticity in what God does through her can only be explained in supernatural terms. Many claim to have gifts from God, and some even use them as their calling card, perhaps charging for services, and many seek to collect large followings of believers who search regularly for comforting words of wisdom or prophecies that fall outside of their relationship with God. Trish is the real deal, yet does not promote herself as such, knowing that God's plan isn't for her fame and fortune, but to teach, heal and cast out demons, speak words of truth and revelation, feeding the malnourished body of Christ. Beware of false teachers and prophets!

When Kingdoms Collide provides the readers enormous insight into various types of spiritual warfare, what intimate communication with the Lord looks like, knowing your identity and authority, and even pain from the shunning others in the body of Christ do once they realize she is authentic and deeply connected to Him! These stories and the view from Trish's eyes will stretch your boundaries of what you believe to be truth about the unseen spirit world. I corroborate each of her accounts during the mission to Songea, Tanzania in 2018. As we prepared for the trip, the power of God was revealed to us, proclaiming that His work will be done. Accurate warnings of enemy opposition and activities were issued to us, and in all cases, we knew that He had gone before us preparing the way. I hope that you enjoy this account of the mission to Africa, but more than that, I pray that God shows you how it truly applies to your life here and now. May God bless you.

~Merlin Hall

Introduction

You are about to embark on a journey in which the presence of darkness directly collides with the spirit of God, during a mission in Africa.

This is my personal story, memorialized for my children, grandchildren, and great grandchildren to come. The interactions were itemized and memorialized in a personal journal that I wrote as each and every day began and concluded.

The spiritual world is real and the battle wages daily, but the truth that is waiting to be witnessed is unchangeable. That truth is the Spirit of God never loses. So, to this extent, I document and tell the truest of stories of the clash of the darkness versus the light. The demonic versus the army and forces of God.

Please note, this is told through my perspective, my experiences, and my heart with the blessing and confirmation of accuracy from my ministry partner and written confirmations from true trusted sources.

All names have been changed and some photos have been purposely distorted, fogged, or pixelated to preserve privacy where needed. My purpose for telling this story from my perspective is not to minimize or overshadow anyone else on the team, or their HUGE contributions to the Kingdom of God, but rather to stay true to my personal experience, my spiritual experience, and my experience with my ministry partner during what **should** have been the most impossible journey I've ever taken.

This was a life changing season that I could never plan for. I grew up knowing the spiritual world, but this trip was to be more than I even thought it ever would be. It was a test, it was a discovery, it was training ground, and it forever altered my identity as a person.

Every day we are on this earth is combat. It's a war between this world and another. This realm and another. A war in which the enemy uses our emotions, our dreads, and our perceived circumstances against us to draw our attention from the greater truth actually found in God. It's a realm that presses in, weighs us down, and influences our moods, actions, and even our perceived identities. It's a continuous war within and a war that wages around us. Navigating this world requires an ocean of faith, but many of us are still on the beach.

God's eyes, hand, and blessing was on this mission that He sent me on long before I set foot on any plane. The evidence was all around, it was just a matter of patience and trust.

We all had our roles to fill. Each member of the team focused on marching according to their individual orders. Each member dovetailing with the assignment of another. Each person having a piece of a puzzle and a purpose that was unique to how they were created and what they were created for.

God long ago told me, "The beginning is written. The end is written. Just live through the pages in between." Yet, God is never caught off guard. He knows the end from the beginning. And in this case, God took time to notify me, His lowly servant of trouble that was to come. Soon it would become clear. With all these uncertainties surrounding us, God's promises, dreams, and visions will be fulfilled.

Earthly logic would have driven me to run and not take the steps necessary to engage my mission. However, I recalled the teachings of my Lord and Savior, "To not commit before you have all the answers is an act against faith," and He reminded me action in obedience without understanding is faith by which we are to live and abide.

2 Corinthians 5:7 (NKJV)

[7] For we walk by faith, not by sight.

I'm in no way suggesting that any others ignore logic, but in my case, I knew I needed to ignore the earthly warnings, dig into the Bible, grab a hold of the hand of my Jesus, and allow God to work me and lead me the way I was created to be led for this mission. Whatever He needed me or wanted me or created me for, I was all His to fulfill His will. Soon I would learn the magnitude of what I experienced. Something I could not properly appreciate for several years to come. And so it began…

Challenge: As you read, take note of each and every collision between the darkness and the light. There are many and the outcomes are each so very unique, just as the Lord we serve is unique. But one thing they each have in common is each one leads us toward something greater…if we are willing to keep going.

How many conflicts can you find? What can you learn from them? What would you do if you were faced with the same here in your own hometown? Would you be prepared and know what to do? I pray that you glean from this what you are intended to glean and that the Lord reveal something to you about your journey to come.

And so it begins...

Just as the world we see, hear, and interact with in daily life seems to enhance our existence, those tangible senses are viewed as our only reality. However, there is more than one reality. Just as radio waves can't been seen but are no less real, the spiritual realm is equally as real. It's all around us. Darting in and out of our lives for different reasons in various seasons, but none the less it is there. Both the influences of the enemy, as well as the inspirations of the heavenly continue to exist.

The spiritual realm is not to be feared but to be respected instead. Not toyed with as in paranormal games or used for entertainment, but instead for us to be aware of, to be heeded, and to remind us of our authority for those who believe in Jesus. Regardless of whether or not we are in touch with that sensory awareness of something from the other side, the entities from the other side are aware of us. They influence our atmosphere, interact with our daily life, and they distract us from goals. The spiritual realm can cause us to sidestep the aspirations of our hearts and the desires that God created within us. We have a purpose for being here, on this earth, right now, in this time...God doesn't make mistakes. You have something that is for the Here and Now and awareness of the spiritual realm is necessary.

As a small child, I became aware of the spiritual. It wasn't something I was taught. Instead, it was something that I sensed. Something inside me knew that what I was experiencing was not just from another realm, but something from the Kingdom of God. Something that we can all have. Holy Spirit.

God's Hidden Preparation

Ready...

In early 2015, I received unexpected urgency in my spirit that urged me into getting my passport renewed, "and do it quickly." As I scratched my head in confusion day after day, this same feeling repeated in my spirit until it had my full attention. In my logical mind, I had no purpose for a passport, but the urgency in my spirit was unrelenting. I truly didn't want to, but I finally told my spouse I needed to get my passport updated and punctuated that need with the word "immediately." It was in that strange urgency that he looked at me with his eyes squinted and head cocked to the side asking, "Why?"

Unfortunately, I didn't have an answer at the time. I looked at him with a face that I knew reflected my own lack of understanding as I replied, "I have NO idea." What I did know was it sounded nutty to my ears, so I know it caused him confusion as well.

You see, I was a homebody. I didn't like to travel, and I had not been out of the country since the early 1980's. I had a major fear of getting too far from home, even here in my hometown. "The closer to home the better," was my motto. Yet this need to get my passport done was tremendous and to me clearly felt as if it was something that was generated outside of my own thoughts, feelings, or desires.

This was something Kingdom that required Kingdom facing attention rather than earthly logic. In addition, it also required my submission and obedience, but that earthly logic just crept right in.

Within a few days, I was thinking like an individual and forgot my Kingdom connection. The result...earthly logic, "There is no reason for this to be so urgent." Yet, I was about to be corrected. The following days were met with ebbs and flows of reminders and unctions that began to just bother me enough that I finally said, "Enough! I'll go."

Upon arrival to the local post office, I was met with the governmental generation of paper trails and frustration consisting of long lines, forms to fill out, and pictures to take, only to be followed up with return trips to the post office and seemingly pointless in direction or information to work off of. I considered quitting. "This is frustrating," I thought, as I rolled my eyes. "Maybe this can wait. Maybe I misunderstood," I pondered, choosing to weigh the urgency in God's unctions. While considering my options to get out of line and go on about my day, I recalled His words and sighed as I moved forward in obedience not knowing that by doing so, I had just **agreed** to be a different kind of soldier in the battlefield for God. My action and choice of submission itself was an act of **agreement** with God's Will. I did not anticipate that my entire spiritual journey was about to expand yet again. The roots that I already had in the Trinity, the spiritual realm, and the Bible were about to multiply. I was about to become rooted in more power and reach greater depths with God I never thought possible in my life.

Years before the Lord moved me into position or directed me to get my passport, I had a vision. In that vision, I saw myself walking off of a plane, onto the tarmac of an airport. Never having deplaned on a tarmac, and having not traveled a whole lot, I was not even aware that being on a tarmac would be an option anywhere. Nevertheless, in that vision, I saw myself walking down a set of stairs next to the engines of a plane and onto a tarmac that seemed very small in comparison to what I know here in the larger cities of the United States. As soon as I received such a vision, I felt my spirit respond with such excitement that it had to be something from above. Something was moving into place and pieces were coming together…"But Father, I don't travel alone and that's not a trip for my husband. Who do I choose?"

Get Set…

After that vision, a few months went by leading us into the following calendar year. As I sat in the pew, God illuminated a man at church that I did not know before that day. As I sat there, God laid in my spirit a message to give this stranger. With a heavy sigh and a little bit of annoyance, I reluctantly approached him. He turned to me. I introduced myself and spoke the words the Lord instructed me to speak, "I would take a bullet for you."

With shock on his face, he stood there in silence for a moment before he said, "I need a moment to process that information."

Laughter exploded out from my lungs as I turned and walked away. Once I walked away, logic caused an assumption that the only time I would be seeing that man again was at church. However, as it so often happens, God doesn't operate off of our human logic, and for that I'm grateful.

After that faithful moment in which I spoke to that man and told him I would take a bullet for him, we were now intertwined on a spiritual level that I could never have planned nor understood.

For many months, event after event, this man who I had never noticed before was now around every corner that I rounded. We became keenly aware of each other and of something complexly illogical that was occurring. Slowly and cautiously, we became friends, but the friendship was deeper than anything on this earth could explain. It was godly, it was safe, it was loving, it was protective, and it was Christ centered.

I smile as I think back at all the faces because for those who were immature in their spiritual growth, it was all so very confusing, and I'd venture to say even concerning. Yet what God puts together no man will separate.

As we continued on our journey, faithful to the illogical process of walking the path that the Lord was leading, before either of us knew what was occurring, we entered a Kingdom connection. We became one of the strongest and enduring ministry partners I could have ever imagined, and with such a crazy path that no one could see coming. God was clear, "together" we are stronger.

God is Setting Up the Launch

Training Ground

As I sat in a meeting with a room full of people, we talked over several subjects. I heard the chatter around the table, but I was paying more attention to the data that was being placed into my spirit. "You are going to Israel."

This wasn't something that was discussed in any format. It wasn't something that I heard in my ears, my head or was even suggested by someone that I had even considered. Instead, it was just a sudden statement of fact that I felt deep in my gut.

Looking back, it must have appeared crazy because the chatter of the room was suddenly silenced by my outward reaction to the inward dialogue I was having with my heavenly Father.

"You are going to Israel."

Again, this was laid into my spirit, as I blurted out the most incredulous, "What?!"

Suddenly, all eyes were on me, and the room went silent. It was at that time I realized I just needed to come into agreement with what God was dropping into my spirit. I needed to **declare** what God said was to come.

With all eyes on me, I spoke the words, "I'm going to Israel." Looking back, I now understand that God was teaching me to walk by Faith, not allowing my circumstances, agendas, and my understanding to determine my future but instead to declare truth solely based on what He dropped into my spirit, with nothing of the flesh to validate my position, to declare His words over my life and know that His words are my future. Walking in Faith, not by sight. (2 Corinthians 5:7)

My husband was in this same meeting at the other end of the conference room, looking at me wide eyed and mouth open in silence. He spoke carefully, "What are you talking about? When? How? With who?" I smiled at him, emboldened by God's promise and added the details that God was plopping into place.

"I'm going to Israel, and it will be with a group, but I don't know anything else."

He looked at me as if I had lost my mind, but I was being taught something and I needed to allow myself to be **teachable.** I had entered a journey that I could not have coordinated.

Suddenly, a trip to Israel as a Minister manifests out of nowhere, but when I returned, unbeknownst to me, I was also now to become an international missionary. God had just taken my **choice** of obedience and launched me into a place I never thought I would ever reach because I never knew it existed. So, when God said to me, "You're going to Africa," I recognized exactly what I was to do. I **declared** it without understanding. This was the new me.

Walking in Purpose

It was time to step into the new me that God designed me to be. Now that I had a working understanding and practical examples of what it means to walk blindly in faith, I was about to plunge in, seemingly well beyond where I thought possible, into the depths of my faith for my own survival.

As God began to move me into a grander scale of trust and relationship with Him, He repeated the words spoken to my spirit, "To not commit before you have all the answers is an act against faith," and "Action in obedience without understanding is the faith by which we are to live."

God loves to make plans for all His children. He is the ultimate event planner and mercifully He makes things stupid proof for me.

Apparently, God is also a travel agent. Because before I knew it, God had laid a vision on me, that unbeknownst to me would be an actual scene that would later play out in real life. The vision was simple but vibrant. It was a vision of a man standing next to me with his hand on my shoulder in prayer while I was on my knees in Africa ministering to a person sitting on the ground. Excitement was percolating in my veins, but it all seemed so far-fetched and impossible, but that is where the Father shines the brightest.

God's Hand

Before I knew it, a few months had passed. I was asked by my pastor's wife to attend a meeting regarding a concert that my church considered participating in. I agreed. At that meeting, I sat next to my Pastor and I said to him, "I need to get to Africa but have no idea how to do it."

He said, "Let me introduce you to someone." We got up and walked over to this very tall man.

My Pastor introduced me and said to the very tall man, "She needs to get to Africa."

Without even a blink of his eye, the man said, "Come with us."

As I said "yes" in agreement, the sound of my own voice saying "yes," without any further information, even startled me. It was as if the Lord had my tongue, and I was just along for the ride. It was an amazingly peaceful feeling. I knew at that moment this was to be an anointed trip. I was a chosen vessel for this trip. Regardless of what others were to do on this trip, He had a plan and a purpose for little ole me to do something that only I was created for. The same was true for all the other team members who were called to provide loving touches in Africa in the way they were created. Kingdom roll call was announced for this mission and my name was called. I gladly stepped into position. This was just so well-choreographed it could only be God's hand clearing the way. I also knew that He was doing something, and warfare was coming. I thought to myself, "Ok Lord, whatever you say," but I had no idea the intensity of the enemy's desperation to keep me out.

It was six months before I was supposed to leave for the mission field. Seemingly, for no apparent reason, I had tripped over my slippers. The same slippers that I had for years. Laying there, I learned I had torn my rotator cuff, created a large tear in my labrum, and dislocated my shoulder. Waiting for the ambulance to arrive, I couldn't help but roll my eyes at the timing of the fall.

The damage was significant, leaving my shoulder unstable and unable to lift or support more than three pounds. The range of motion was almost nonexistent. In the following months, my shoulder was diagnosed as "frozen."

As I look back, I have to chuckle a bit. It's one thing to say, "I believe in the power, protection, and sovereignty of the Father," and it's another to actually believe it so deeply that I left the country with that driving my entire mindset.

As crazy as it might sound, I didn't have it repaired. I made the conscious decision to hold off on my surgery until I was back state side. That meant I was going into enemy territory and into a third world country with one working arm and shoulder.

In the days leading up to my departure, I made an effort to get dressed for work. As I tried to get my shirt over my head, my husband asked, "How are you going to drag two large suitcases in and out of airports, transports, and steps if you can't even get your own shirt on?"

"I don't know, but somehow I'm not worried about it," was my only reply. I know it sounded crazy, but I was really at peace.

If that wasn't enough, God upped the ante in my faith. I learned that most of what is eaten in the territory we were going into was plant based. With an allergy to onion, garlic, and citrus, sarcasm bubbled up in my mind, "What could possibly go wrong?!" Yep, I was being an idiot in the flesh but obedient in the spirit.

During this time, I was completely unaware of what the Lord was doing with Doyle. The Lord was working on him, and he was keeping it quiet. You see, Doyle had a long history of successes in his life and had been very protective of those successes. This led to a very powerful presence that had a tendency to take command of any situation. The Lord was actively placing him and me into proper position for something that was for the Kingdom, and that required obedience.

Doyle went before the Lord and asked as he did regularly, "What am I supposed to be doing now? What ministry am I supposed to be doing now? What is my next point of focus?"

It was then that the Lord conveyed an answer that he did not anticipate, "Support her and her ministry."

The Lord was putting Doyle in position to support and protect. It wasn't something that I asked for. It wasn't something we even discussed. It was something that God instructed. Now Doyle had some decisions to make and some of his own adjustments to consider. If he chose to obey, that would put him in a different role than he had ever been in. But the Lord knew that I would need a strong male presence in my ministry, and he knew exactly who the man for the job was…Doyle.

Warnings Begin

Six weeks prior to leaving, I began having dreams. Two dreams to be specific. One indicating that a short haired, dark haired woman was going to attack me spiritually in an attempt to drive a wedge between myself and my Doyle to destroy our ministry. I conveyed to Doyle that the goal of this mystery woman was to try and tear down the partnership that God established, challenge my ethics and morals, to create pain and doubt within me, and attempt to wield power that she does not actually have.

In other words, the enemy was sending one of his own into our camp. In fact, God not only knew about it in advance (since He knows the end of all things from the beginning), He also permitted it and may have even in some ways orchestrated it, just as He did in Job.

The second dream of a dark haired, dark skinned woman was going to attack me spiritually and physically.

It took me a moment to really digest such information. Thinking to myself, "Ok God, so you want me to knowingly and willingly go into a country where I'm going to be attacked emotionally, physically, and spiritually, more than once?! By more than one person?!"

The Lord replied, "But there will be no lasting damage and it's not your fight to manage."

You see, in the dreams, the first mystery woman was all too pleased to show her face but concealed her eyes with sunglasses each time, indicating that she was hiding who she truly was. She was prideful but gloated in getting close to me. When she felt comfortable in close proximity to me, she would wait until my head was turned before she would reach for something that didn't belong to her.

I knew with this one, no matter how nice she seemed it was an act and a lie. In other words, she would be lurking. I was "expected" to consider her as a friend, and she was an opportunist. Her face proudly displayed a pride filled smirking smile that conveyed disdain for me but a conscious effort to conceal it.

In the dream, the pride filled woman would wear a scarf that at times hid her face, but only to be blow off long enough for me to see her. Each time she was looking at me. My heavenly Father was warning me, this woman was pride filled, selfish, and on a mission. The target…me.

My ministry partner also had dreams of this same woman who was showing up with sunglasses. In his dream she was in a vehicle while driving in a lane next to his vehicle. She was just slightly behind him. Doyle and I realized that not only would this woman be targeting me out of pride but that she would be on his tail, watching and even trying to distract. The most interesting portion of each of our dreams was that this pride filled, arrogant woman would be going in the same direction as the both of us, but with clear and opposing agendas and motives.

The second woman in the second dream was full of rage and wanted me hurt if not dead. She was sent by someone higher, and she was going to follow the directions…no matter what.

This was starting to sound like one "hell" of a trip.

The most recent dream caused me to question if I was doing the right thing by going. When people learned of the latest warning, most began to try and instill their own fears onto my decisions. "You can't go, God's warning you not to go!"

With religion running through my thoughts and people around me fueling them, I began to question my own connection with God, "Am I wrong God? Did I not hear you correctly? Did I misjudge the way you connect with me? The way you relate to me?"

I had to take a few days to silence all the voices and questions that made their way into my day. I asked the Lord again, "Should I avoid the trip?" It was silly for me to ask such a question. It's a trip that He laid in my spirit, one that He put on my heart and arranged for me to take. A trip that He created and designed me for. And it was people that were causing me to waver. I refused to cower and continued to ask my Father God, "Should I avoid the trip to Africa?"

His answer was simple, "No." But He warned me further by laying in my spirit the words of truth, "When you are the most vulnerable, she will attack. She's calculating." It wasn't comfortable to receive from the all-knowing God that I would be "isolated" in every way and that was part of her design.

Each woman had an agenda, but God was already in motion. "Lord what am I to do?

As quickly as I asked it, I received in my spirit, "Stay low" and "stay aware."

That was when I realized this wasn't about me. I was just the one assigned to walk this mess out. It was about what God was going to do with this mystery woman. It was about God showing me and those who were not blind the magnitude of His love of people and the power of His presence. For one woman, I'm just the bait. For the other, I'm just the vessel.

Again, I updated Doyle and continued. As the time grew closer, people whom I had trusted began to try and influence my decision to go more and more. Again, they insisted that either I abort the mission or pray the attack away from me. Again, I heard their religious understanding conveyed to me to "pray against it" or "rebuke it." But by this time, I knew better. If anything, I chose to rebuke the religious thinking.

I sat down and asked my Lord and savior, "Father, how am I supposed to respond? How am I supposed to feel?"

The Lord was immediate in His response as He reminded me, "Jesus knew Judas was coming but He did not rebuke Him." That was a deep statement. One that still rings in my thoughts.

God warned me and He was permitting the attack. My choices were either find peace in knowing God was fully in control or believe that the devil was more powerful than God.

I could excuse myself from the mission out of the fear of the unknown and question God's control. I could have chosen to control my destiny or let God walk me through my purpose.

I chose to believe in my relationship with God and His loving coverage over me…no matter what.

It felt weighty.

The Mine Field

Before we knew it, we were scheduled on flights to Africa, headed for Songea, Tanzania, with a team of eight. The film crew followed on a later flight.

As we headed for the airport, I felt the lift from the flesh to the spirit and welcomed what was to come. So, there we were...headed to a place called Songea, 297 miles from what seemed to be the furthest rural "airstrip" in the southern highland region of Tanzania.

This was not going to be a trip of comfort for Doyle and me. Don't get me wrong, we would be treated well, but the assignment my ministry partner and I had was different than the rest of the team. We would have no back up, and we would have no contact with anyone else on the team at times. It was truly Doyle's faith and my faith that would carry us through.

Combat Begins

The first day of travel took us from the state of Missouri to Toronto, Canada and then to Addis Ababa, Ethiopia. Doyle and I have both flown nationally and internationally without issue in the past or leading up to this flight. Everything was fine…until we left from Canada to Ethiopia, when we left the continent.

During the flight to Addis Ababa, something didn't feel right. It was as if the air pressure in the cabin was not enough. My head was pounding. I looked around at others and noticed no issues with anyone else. People were going about their business without any visible signs of distress. Doyle was also quietly experiencing the same, confirming something was abnormal, but somehow it made sense.

You see, Doyle and I are Kingdom united as one in this mission and any attack that was to be placed against me would indirectly affect him and vice versa. As time wore on, I realized that my breathing was getting more and more shallow, so sleeping was not the best idea. I started getting very lightheaded, and the ever-increasing crushing pain was beginning to affect my ability to think clearly.

I asked the Lord to show me what was the action required to combat this attack. Doyle, as if he knew I was struggling, had already reached over and prayed for me, but there was something else going on. I realized something unholy was pressing in on me and my partner and it had to be broken. Principality and Powers perhaps. Regardless, he and I were both made aware of its presence. Something knew we were coming, and it didn't like it.

I lasted about ten hours, with each hour getting harder and harder to think and breathe. It was a feeling that could only be described as if I was having an aneurism. My vision was starting to be affected and I still felt as if there was an elephant on my chest and there wasn't enough air. Somewhere around that tenth hour, I saw that three members of our ministry team had congregated in front of where I was sitting on the plane, about three rows up at the bulkhead. I hesitated about getting up, not sure if my legs or my head were going to allow me to reach them. To be honest, I really didn't want anyone (except Doyle) to know I was in distress, but I recognized that this was an attack of a principality or power. This was not an average spirit, and I needed some Kingdom power in action. It was time to draw some boundaries.

Boundaries Drawn

Public Declaration of the Power of Jesus!

I got up from my seat and approached them. I advised the three female team members of the pain I was in, and without a moment of thought, intuitively we all joined hands. We entered into an open, public, unashamed, unbridled, very vocal, prayer to Jesus to heal my head pain. Almost immediately, my head began to clear, and I was able to think without pain.

Noticeably, two of the three women were clear in their prayer against the enemy. However, conspicuously, one remained questionably silent. Instead, she opened her eyes and looked at me. We held each other's gaze and something about it put a check in my spirit. Unknowingly, I was witnessing a precursor to what was to come. A desire to minimize my effectiveness and even damage me.

"I must have misread that. She can't be out to get me," I thought to myself. I continued to wrestle in my thoughts, "She's known for her prayer and her leadership at churches." Why would she not pray for me and why did she look at me that way?

Overall, we drew plenty of attention as three out of the four of us naturally rolled into our prayer languages loudly and boldly with the understanding that we were being watched by people all across the plane.

Once we were finished with the prayer, I took a moment to assess my pain. To my relief, the pain was no longer present, and I could breathe clearly. The air felt different instantly. My thoughts were clear and focused. After ten hours of attack, we just broke the oppressive spirit that was on that plane with one unified prayer. Looking back, this should have been a pretty good indication of the enemy's efforts to stop what we were about to do, and the lengths of which God will go to preserve His mission, which I was walking in with total obedience.

Doyle and I talked here and there throughout the flight as he sat cattycorner from me across the aisle. Unbeknownst to us, there was a lady sitting in front of me listening the entire time. She turned to me and began to cry. She said her name was Melanie and she was overwhelmed with joy because she had come from Ethiopia and knew the need for people to know the name, life, and death of Jesus.

The clear indication of emotion in her wording impacted me as I saw the depth of what she was trying to convey. I was so moved that I recorded her wording in writing the day she spoke to me. This stranger went out of her way to tell us that what we were doing was beautiful because they were never taught about Jesus growing up. She explained that her life was a mess until she came to know Jesus. Melanie turned in her seat to look at me squarely in the eye. I could see she wanted me to clearly hear something that she felt she had to say. As I leaned forward, it was almost surreal as she said the words in a hushed tone, "The Spirit is with you." But as if that wasn't enough, she repeated it again with more emphasis, "The Spirit is with you." She held my gaze as if the words were not enough. She needed me to see it in her eyes. There was information being exchanged in just the intensity of her eyes as if she wanted me to see into the depth of her mind.

I shook my head in acknowledgment of what she was trying to convey as I said, "Yes" and "Thank you."

Yet the intensity was not over, and the moment had not yet passed. Melanie spoke it again as if she could not convey the importance of what she was saying. Her accent getting thicker as her attempt to keep her intensity under control, "No, I mean it. The Spirit is with you." It was a moment that I will not forget. She was delivering a message that seemed outside of this world and I saw it for what it was. She was a messenger. Something about this trip just turned from an anointed mission trip to a supernatural expose.

Melanie motioned with her hand to make sure she conveyed that the message was for both of us when she spoke it the last time. Appearing as if she was trying to tell us something about Doyle and I that she did not have words for. Doyle and I looked at each other, each recognizing something was occurring in that moment and the rest of the plane was none the wiser. Melanie asked permission to pray for us. When we asked why this stranger would want to pray for us, she conveyed, "You're going to need it." Doyle and I knew this was an appointment and the message was just delivered.

The Mission Begins

GO!!

The last flight of the day took us from Addis Ababa to a fabulous place called Dar Es Salaam, Tanzania. These long flights were tedious, so out of self-preservation I decided to get up and stretch my legs while Doyle went to use the restroom. Upon my return, I unexpectedly decided to take Doyle's seat instead of my own. He came back and quickly took my seat and with an ease of a seasoned minister, that is when he met my seatmate, Ahmed.

Ahmed sat quietly reading the Quran and on occasion looked up and out the window to mouth his prayers with deep contemplation.

Up to that point, my seatmate was quiet, only sending awkward glances my direction every now and then. He was a Muslim man, and I was a Christian woman. He was unsure of his role and what was acceptable. However, when Doyle sat down, Ahmed relaxed.

Doyle easily invited him into a conversation toward where the Holy Spirit was leading him. They spoke of life, mission, and faith as dialogue about our Jesus and Holy Spirit fell easily from Doyle's lips. Ahmed began to "feel" the words that my partner had spoken. It was as if something ignited in Ahmed, and without prompting, Ahmed suddenly began to ask for an explanation of what he was feeling. He wanted to understand. There was an excitement in his eyes, in his spirit, and he was searching for the answer as to what that feeling was. It was then that Doyle explained to him he was feeling the Holy Spirit. Doyle paused and watched as Ahmed was visibly moved by this intimate response by the Holy Spirit. Ahmed held unapologetic tears in his eyes as his spirit recognized the power of the Holy Spirit, while holding the Quran in his hand.

When it felt like the time was right, I returned to my seat. As I looked at the book he was reading, I noticed it was beautifully ornate, but I didn't understand the illustrations or writing. I knew it to be the Quran, so I asked him to show me what it looked like from his perspective. I wanted to see through his eyes and understanding so that I could learn how to talk to him.

Before I knew it, he was teaching me about what it said, how it was read, and the meanings of each illustration. What started as an awkward long flight turned into such an easy beautiful conversation.

Almost immediately, Ahmed asked me why I was going to Africa.

I smiled and responded, "To teach about Jesus." We began to talk about Holy Spirit, and I watched as the concentration washed over his face.

He didn't even try to hide his interest in all that occurred in Jesus' short 33 years of life. Ahmed openly conveyed his intrigue into learning the details of the death of Jesus and was visibly overwhelmed at the resurrection story. His face is imprinted on my memory as he just stared, not sure what to say, and considered all that was said. I could almost see him recalling the physical and spiritual response he had to the presence of the Holy Spirit when Doyle was sitting here.

There was no doubt in what I was witnessing. Something was coming together in his understanding. The feeling, the experience, the understanding, and now the connection. He was receiving truth and his spirit knew it. His eyes deepened from the seeds that were just planted. The word was taking on a life of its own. God was finding His people and setting them in front of us. Or in this case, next to us. So, it began...

Vision Fulfilled

Confirmations Begin

Before I knew it, the plane landed in Ethiopia. Almost immediately, I smiled and began giggling. We didn't taxi to a gate. There wasn't a well-organized walkway onto a quiet concourse of an attached airport.

I grabbed the small bag that I could carry with my one good arm and began walking down a narrow stairwell from the body of the plane and onto the primitive unfamiliar ground. We gathered as a group and collectively walked past the planes and into a building to find the next steps for the next leg of our journey. There was much confusion waiting for us as we were instructed to weigh our luggage.

Before us was a large, oversized scale that looked beautifully awkward and equally primitive. As we placed luggage onto the scale, the arm of the scale spun with the calculation. As I stood there waiting for my luggage to be slugged on top of the antiquated scale that looked like something out of the 1800's, I suddenly realized the vision was being fulfilled from long ago.

Recalling the simplicity of me walking down the stairs of a small plane onto the tarmac of a primitive airport warmed my spirit. God had given me notice of what was to come. At the time, I thought it was a silly vision, something that was just in my imagination. In such a technology-based world, I assumed such an event would never come to pass. Thoughts like, "Why would I be on a tarmac?" and "That kind of experience doesn't even exist…right?" These thoughts attempted to discount or minimize God's promises at the time, but on this day, I saw them playing out in front of me.

God knew this would be part of my experience and it served to confirm that I was in the right place at the right time. God was moving and I was moving with Him. In unison.

Adjusting to the Atmosphere

Stepping Back in Time

After much travel and shuffling from one place to another, we finally arrived at our resting place for the evening in Dar Es Salaam, Tanzania. The hotel was surrounded by metal spiked gates and fencing that rose up nine to ten feet in height. When we asked about the reason for the fencing, we were told it was for our protection.

Regardless of how tired we were or the fact that we were choosing to go outside of the fencing, we decided to wander the area to experience the atmosphere by immersing ourselves in it.

It was almost surreal. The streets were made of uneven dirt and discarded dirty water which we navigated carefully in our very American clothing and shoes. Needless to say, we did not blend in very well as we walked the predominantly Muslim streets of the daily life of Africa. Vendors and chickens lined the streets among the holes and ditches that were big enough to swallow a car. Every street was lined with people, produce, wares for sale and motorcycles. The entire scene was fantastic, exhilarating, and peaceful.

The locals were open in their curiosity as they watched us and assessed the reason for our presence. I smiled as we allowed ourselves to be studied and sized up with every step we took.

We continued our stroll as we jumped over holes, smiled, and waved at everyone. We laughed and bounced in an apologetic joyful course that had no real direction for the moment. Doyle and I took in the most incredible sights and smells. Lean-tos made of scrap tin and wood that had dried fish laying out in the sun. Tin or thatched huts that had no doors, no plumbing, no windows, and no electricity but had two sewing machines with hundreds of bolts of brightly colored fabric proudly displayed in them caused my sensibilities to swim with questions and intrigue. Two women working quickly to finish projects working so diligently they only looked up to yell out something in Swahili to another.

People kept to themselves for the most part, going about their daily activities of selling food, fixing motorcycles, or just sitting and waiting for someone to approach so they could sell their wares. I noticed there wasn't a lot of chatter or laughter coming from any of the shops. It felt very strange. However, I recognized the principality and power that was hovering over this place. The oppression, the confusion, the weight of the witchcraft was present, but there was much to come.

As Doyle and I walked, I noticed a man wearing portions of Muslim attire watching us intently. We were clearly Christians as I wore my cross proudly around my neck. No one from our group really knew where we were but we were both ok with that. The man in Muslim attire actively began to parallel with us from across the roadway. He was sizing us up, but we were not concerned. We were on a mission assigned from the Lord and the enemy was slithering around us.

Rather than acting as if we didn't see him, we chose to smile and wave to him. Needless to say, we didn't get much of a response, if any.

Our presence was agitating him, and he was responding. As he continued to watch Doyle and I, he began to angle his body toward us with a gradual but intentional descent and interception. His face held no smile, but he was clearly determined to make contact. Throughout our stroll through this foreign land and newly discovered area, Doyle and I walked side by side as we would in any other setting, but the Holy Spirit was warning me that there was danger approaching, specifically to me. Without hesitation, I heeded the warning choosing to cross over to the other side of my partner, affectively placing distance between myself and the approaching local.

The local was now within a foot of us. So, apparently, it was time for a conversation. He spoke broken English and we had no translator, so we began a careful dialogue to determine the man's intent. Through a series of gestures and broken words we determined that he was guarding his territory. He was curious about who we were and why we were there, but more than that, he wanted to know what was happening.

He indicated that something felt different in the atmosphere as we were walking by and he didn't like it. It was unfamiliar and he wanted answers. It wasn't just that we were dressed differently. It wasn't just that we were a different color. It was the light that we carried.

Doyle began to speak to him, "We are here from the United States of America, and we are here to teach about Jesus."

The man smiled and indicated he wanted to know more about "this Jesus." Doyle obliged but made sure we kept the conversation unthreatening. The man responded with loose and non-committal responses but invited us to his shop later, if we were interested. It was a strange mix of genuine curiosity and ill intent toward us that punctuated the stir in the atmosphere, and we were right smack in the middle of it. As I looked around, all eyes were on Doyle and me talking to this man. All faces knew something was amiss, but they were not about to get involved. I motioned to Doyle it was time to go. He responded quickly and with ease as he assured the man that we were appreciative of his hospitality and gently dismissed him so that we could safely make our way back to the secured walls of the hotel. Once back to the hotel, we separated to enter our own independent rooms. I looked out the windows and took in from the second-floor room what I couldn't see from the ground.

I observed a man out of my window. His home was made of tin, concrete, and scraps of wood. He was in his backyard and actively dipping water out of filthy troughs and puddles, putting

it into plastic containers. It struck me, for the most part, that I have taken for granted the access to clean water when others are using water that is black, gray, or brown. What was even more telling was at the time we were there in Africa, it was no longer in the rainy season and was actually into their winter months. I suddenly understood that the water he was collecting was not from rain but more than likely runoff from the local vendors as they dumped their dirty water waste into the streets.

The reality of survival and the inner strength in a will to survive was right in front of me. Not waiting on someone else to make their life better but working with what they had. I had respect for the people in this area. I was here for reasons that were unknown to me, but well known by my Father.

Strangely, I felt at home in Africa. All warnings suggested I should be concerned, or even scared, yet there was no fear in me. Our hotel was heavily protected indicating that there were threats, yet I felt none.

It was apparent that there were regular and significant dangers in the area that were the cause of a well thought out and constructed protective barrier system that consisted of six-foot walls made of concrete and steel with spikes that were topped with eight rows of electrified fencing. This was clearly serious protection from enemy attack. In the flesh, a person might want to let their minds wander as to why those measures were necessary? What dangers were we being protected from? While my earthly eyes knew what was in front of me, my spiritual eyes saw the love in the hearts of the people. Fear had no room in my head. Wandering the streets unarmed with just one other person seemed so contrary to the protective measures that were clearly put into place to keep us safe. Yet that is what I preferred.

There was no time to waste in weighing the potential dangers that were glaringly in front of us. What God was doing mattered more to me than any physical circumstances. I was committed to what I was assigned to do, walking in total faith and unyielding to what the eyes of the flesh might gravitate toward. The mission was in movement and God was preparing the way.

Settling into my room that night, I noticed I wasn't alone. There was a lizard that was cruising around the walls and clearly at home doing it. I couldn't help but laugh joyfully at the simplicity of this place. Nothing fancy but everything that was needed. A bed, a desk, a chair, and a fan. No elevators, no carpet, no fancy towels, no complementary shampoo, or other luxuries that we have become accustomed to in the United States. What was there was just exactly what was needed.

I began to settle in for the night and as I did, it became apparent that Larry the Lizard felt he needed to also settle in for the night. I considered my options. However, I quickly drew a boundary with a no reptile policy. The look of the hotel staff was a cross between confusion as to why I couldn't get rid of Larry myself and why his presence was a problem, but I held firm that the lizard needed to be evicted.

Two people came up to my room and I watched as they began running around, climbing on furniture and my luggage to try and get Larry out of sight so he would also be out of mind. Larry was pretty quick though; he wasn't going without a fight, and he was going to wear out these humans if it was the last thing he did. And it was. I laughed so hard at the antics that were created by one little eight-inch lizard as he was chased around the room that we were joined by other members of our team wondering what the cause of all the racket was. Before we knew it, we were all laughing.

Once poor Larry the lizard was "removed" from my room, I took my shower, being careful not to get any water in my mouth or eyes. While I had no fear, I also knew that God had gone ahead of me and created predestined meetings to encounter, and

my responsibility was to be diligent in my decisions so I can be as healthy and clear headed as possible. God had the rest.

The showers have no doors. As a matter of fact, there is no division of shower, toilet or sink at all. It's very difficult to explain, but I've provided photos later to better illustrate it. Turning on the light wasn't an option as the exposed wiring above the sink and the light bulb that hung from it right next to the shower didn't give me a lot of comfort.

I observed the flooring before setting my foot on it. Lizards were cute, but not in my shower. When looking around, I noticed everything was glass tile. Glass, open electric wires, and water…"hmmm…" I laughed (which is something I do a lot) shrugged my shoulders and thought to myself, "So let do this."

Needless to say, I set out to shower quickly as the tank in my room didn't look to have much capacity of hot water and it was getting dark in the bathroom.

Culturally speaking, the scene made me giggle. So…no door, exposed electric wires while the electric was on, glass tile flooring with water flowing on it and oh by the way, don't get water in your mouth and watch for mosquitoes.

My thoughts focused on God's presence, "God you are so funny."

You know how people say, "be careful" before they leave? Well, that wasn't an option, so I laughed.

I opened my eyes while washing the shampoo and layers of travel out of my hair. I noticed about a foot above my head was an open window. Well beyond my reach. I continued my shower as I mused at the irony. Mosquitos love water. Yes, it technically had a screen but is it really a screen if there are huge holes in it?

It was then that I smiled as I recalled my decision not to take malaria medications. I had an internal battle when it came to the suggested malaria medications that we were told to take. Everything inside of me felt the Holy Spirit asking me to trust Him instead of leaning on my own understanding. I felt I was being asked to not take the medications which seemed crazy, as if I was being tossed into the lion's den and looking for Jesus in the flames. But I knew my Father's voice in my spirit, so I chose to trust in that relationship.

As far as I know, I was the only one on this trip that chose to forgo the medications (unsure what my ministry partner chose). Regardless, it would be ok.

NOTE: Forgoing medications is not a decision I would suggest anyone else make. This is just what I chose.

It was dusk and I chose not to turn on my bathroom lighting for obvious reasons, so I finished my shower and dressed quickly. This task turned into a bit of a challenge since everything in the bathroom was wet and no place to sit but the toilet with no lid...but I was tired so anything would be ok.

That evening, as I watched the sun fade away and the darkness close in, I found myself acutely aware of my surroundings. Although the sun was down and it was getting very late, the world around me was wide awake. Dar es Salaam was buzzing with activity very late into the night. Since I am a light sleeper, I didn't try to force sleep. Instead, I just sat there and captured my thoughts and prayers. Being intentional about my time there seemed to make the most sense. It was then that I continued my journal from which this book came.

Stay Awake

After a bit of journaling, I found myself yawning and ready to settle into the slumber that I had hoped I would find. Sleeping in an unfamiliar place is always a challenge. However, quite some time later, I found the slumber that I sought after.

As I began to slide into a dream filled state, I was jolted awake at the sound of something unknown and unidentified repeatedly tapping me on the face. For a while, I ignored the unknown annoyance, surmising it as just a moth. I swatted at it in the darkness several times but realized it was going to remain unrelenting.

This tapping would touch my cheek, then chin, then nose or forehead and repeat in some random order until out of frustration I reached over and flipped on the light.

The light came on with a "click" just in time to see something hazy and black in flight leaving the vicinity of my face. It seemed to just disappear without any real direction or exit point. As I sat up and looked around, I considered the options. Maybe a large moth? No, much too big. A bat maybe? No, a little bit too small. And regardless, where did it go? I decided to go with logic as I checked under my pillow, under my bed, and rolled back the sheet. It was nowhere to be found, but the most irritating part was that there was no place for it to go. It vanished into thin air right before my eyes.

I thought to myself, "Ok, so something doesn't want me to sleep, but I'm going to get sleep." I rolled my eyes at the lame attempt of the enemy, shook my head, and flipped my light back off.

As I laid back, I was peaceful in my spirit, not a worry in my thoughts but feeling very, very tired. I drifted to sleep. Before I knew it, my sleep was once again interrupted in the middle of the night with the persistent repetition of chants and prayers from the local mosque. The prayers were clearly through a public announcement system that continued throughout the night and well into the early morning hours.

Needless to say, I was now wide awake. As I just laid there and listened, (or tried not to listen) to the prayers that filtered through the darkness and floated through the air, I found myself praying over the people. I found myself asking for God's clarity for the people and for a pathway to Jesus to be revealed to each and every one that feels the call of the Lord on their hearts.

Each time the mosque began its prayers, my response was the same...prayer over the people. It seemed to be every couple of hours but after sleep deprivation kicked in, I no longer heard it.

Unfortunately, I didn't get much sleep with the constant interruptions. But there was a calm, peaceful wash of God's coverage that flooded the atmosphere. I'll never know if my payers reached any one person, but what I do know is God is good.

The next morning, I mentioned to my sweet friend, an Evangelist that I will refer to as "Danielle," about the tapping on my face I had experienced the night before. Danielle's room was right next to mine. As I told her about the tapping, she locked at me and informed me that about that same time she had felt something watching her from the direction of my room.

"Really..." I said, partially pleased that someone else experienced something besides just me and partially intrigued to learn of her experience. She began to go into detail of what she experienced and ended her explanation just as I thought she would. Danielle, being the strong intercessor she is, replied with, "I rebuked it." There was nothing left to do but laugh…this was just the beginning, but we were up for the journey.

Breakfast was being prepared as we talked, and the repacking followed as we prepared to climb back into another vehicle to head to the next flight. The journey continues.

The Convergence

The next flight was much smaller and louder, but so much fun. The further into Tanzania we flew, the smaller the transportation got and it was so enjoyable. This flight, I sat next to my ministry partner (Doyle). We were just chatting away during our two-hour flight when all of a sudden, I noticed something felt strange. I sat at the window by the engines midway down the plane. My gaze was drawn to the curtain divider that separated the front of the plane from the area where the water carts are stocked. I couldn't see anything manifesting in the physical so I asked, "Lord, show me what you want me to see."

He did exactly that, as I continued to look into that direction an image came to my mind's eye and suddenly right there in front of us was a black entity silently hovering in place. It would be best described as a ghost like mist, or what is commonly referred to as an apparition, but not. It felt very male in energy and very angry. So, there we were, just my ministry partner, me, and Mr. Angry spirit just hovering there, glaring towards the back of the plane.

Perplexed as to what Mr. Angry spirit was looking at, I followed its gaze and looked back at the people behind us. I saw nothing out of the ordinary. Just people being people in a loud and cramped plane.

Regardless, I felt I should say something, so I mentioned to Doyle what was going on. He looked at me and responded, "I don't ever doubt you, but you're sure it's not your imagination?"

I smiled. He should know me better by now. He's experienced enough with me but he's also the pragmatist so for his comfort I played devil's advocate and said with a grin of confidence on my face, "Well if it's God, it will be confirmed. If it's my imagination, it won't be. It's that simple"

Because it was so loud, we couldn't really discuss anything further, so he looked into the direction of Mr. Angry spirit, turned to look at me, and nodded in acknowledgment. What we didn't know was what was to come from that or why Mr. Angry spirit was even there.

As the flight continued, the entity got more and more agitated but we, being accustomed to the spiritual world, just carried on with our lives laughing, joking, and enjoying the beef jerky I had stashed in my carry on.

What Doyle and I were not aware of was, prior to the flight, there was a "situation." You see...this "airport" was very small, very rural, antiquated, and ill equipped to handle international travelers in an efficient way. As a result, one of the locals was unhappy with the Americans, especially the American women in attendance.

Doyle and I were initially unaware of the angry encounter because of our approximation to the actual confrontation. When the team arrived at the airport, each member was scattered just a bit. We were either instructed by their staff to proceed into lines or instructed to wait off to the side. During this time, our passports were gathered, paperwork was exchanged, validated, and verified. Those of us that were sent off to the side did not hear or know of the conflict that was building.

Apparently, the conflict stemmed from a local man who was annoyed with the team being in front of him in line. I don't know if it was because we were Americans, some of us were Caucasian, half the team was female, or if it was because we were Christians, but from what I was told, he was verbally aggressive and loud with a woman on our team that crossed in front of him when trying to comply with airport directions.

I do recall seeing the desk and the lines of people facing the desk. Although we were separated, we maintained eye contact, when possible, to keep from being permanently separated as the leadership held all of our documentation.

There was a question posed by the airport personnel. However, in order to answer the question, the woman on our team needed to approach the desk, but that required the action of crossing in front of the man. The female leadership of our team assessed the situation and told this team member to cross in front of him regardless of his statements. The man became more verbally aggressive toward the group. From what I was told, it was downhill from there. In other words…Mr. Angry spirit was confirmed.

Gratefully, I was blissfully oblivious and caught up in all the movement and activity around our immediate position and never saw a thing, even though it occurred less than ten feet from me.

Grateful that this airport was so noisy, I was told that the angry man, who was not shy about running his mouth regarding any issue concerning women or Americans, boarded the plane with us and apparently headed directly to the back of the plane, never quite calming down from his little tirade.

In hindsight, it all made sense. The flesh often responds to what is going on in the spiritual realm. That man was influenced by this entity. This man was just a toy for the spirit to play with. Whether by choice, by lack of understanding, lack of caring, ignorance or carelessness, this man was participating with the spirit that chose him.

Again, the flesh and the spirit were converging. Once I heard the story of the angry man, I smiled and spoke the word to Doyle that let me know I was on the right track, "Confirmed." Confirmation of what was seen in the spirit, and what occurred in the flesh...this was going to get interesting.

Exercise in Humility and Humor

We arrived at our destination without much issue. As we disembarked, we moved toward where we would be picked up by the next vehicle and headed to the place we were to sleep for the night.

It was getting late, and the hotel room had very little or dim lighting. Nothing like being in a foreign country, with unfamiliar surroundings and very little lighting. Surveying my surroundings in the ever-dimming light, I decided to get my room set up for my shower and the night while I had some daylight to see. I found the light switch and gave it a flick of the wrist. "Click!"

To my surprise, nothing much changed. I looked up and the light was on, but my room was a deep pink leaving very little for the lighting to reflect. Instead, the walls just absorbed the light like a sponge.

Smiling as I acknowledged embracing the journey, I walked into my bathroom. Laughter impulsively broke through my lips. It was dark in my bathroom and my bedroom, but the light was still streaming through the one window I had. After settling in, I checked out the bathroom. Walking around the corner and lifting my foot to go up two steps, I turned and was faced with another bathroom that made me giggle.

Above: My bathroom

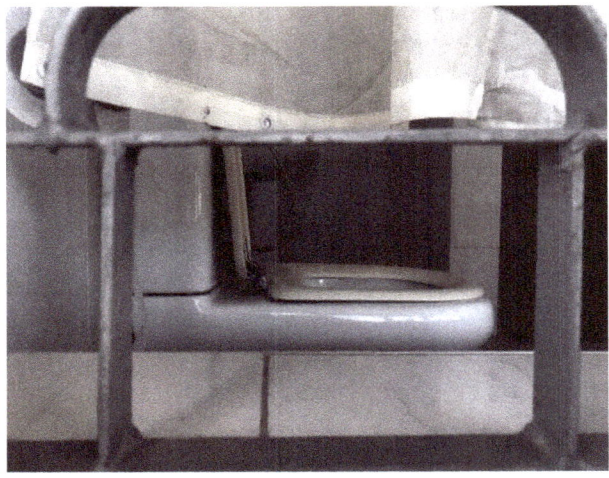
Above: My friends bathroom view from the public balcony above.

It was déjà vu only a bit more entertaining. There was the standard handheld shower head that remained directly above the toilet. I tested the water to see if it was rusty and to make sure it worked. I quickly found that the tank was filled with extremely cold water. I turned it back off and hoped it would warm up and wiped off the new very wet toilet with the very weak streamed bidet. "Not to worry, I thought to myself, "I didn't need a good bidet because I had a conveniently placed shower head to use!" There was no choice but to laugh out loud at this one and no... nothing to separate them.

I turned to close the door so that I could use the bathroom when I clearly heard in my spirit, "Do NOT close that door." You see, hearing in the spirit has nothing to do with hearing words in your mind or with your ears. Hearing in your spirit is more of an intuitive understanding, clarity, or piece of information that feels like a warning in your gut and comes from an unknown or unseen source that does not necessarily match the physical circumstances around you.

Receiving that warning, I took my hand off the bathroom door and surveyed the door itself. It looked fine, maybe I heard that wrong. Not chancing it, I left the door open while I finished my business.

Looking around, I noticed an added element of difficulty. This time there was an added twist to the journey. I couldn't help but think, "Hmmm, what is wrong with this picture?"

The fact that the shower head was also facing an open window that didn't close wasn't the issue. The larger issue was the partial piece of cloth covering the window that was the only barrier between my vulnerable state and the village's main gathering place for gasoline.

BUT I could watch the sunset while I showered!

NOTE: Although it's hard to achieve the full perspective from the photo, the cloth stopped at my navel and the wall resumed at my thighs. The peek-a-boo gap being about a foot to a foot and a half.

I wandered out of my room to figure out what was next in the plan. Some of us walked out to a public balcony to talk about dinner. One of our core members showed up with a menu that we all looked at to get an idea of what we might be able to eat that evening. The sun was going down but still plenty of light to survey our surroundings. It was delightful to watch the world move past us as we just stood there and observed. Yes, we had five rows of what appeared to be electric fencing between our team and the rest of the world, but it was intriguing none the less.

As the sun receded and our stomachs assumed dinner might be ready soon, we proceeded to wander around a bit to get familiar with our surroundings before all converging in the room we were to eat in. There was a conscious effort in walking as the three stories of stairs were very irregular and uneven, being careful to not misjudge the height and placement of the next step. I found myself making a mental note of where to put my feet as there were no lights in the stairwells at all. Some steps were no more than 3 inches tall, and others were 18 inches.

In awe, I watched as the teenage girls dragged luggage up and down these stairs repeatedly as part of their hospitality as I fought the urge to offer to help. I knew this action to assist us was their custom, and selfishly, I also reasoned I wasn't going to risk my shoulder. This was another opportunity for me to practice humility.

P. Frederick

On the "Lighter" Side

The African food was interesting. Fish soup was literally a fish, eyes and all, laid inside a bowl with the head and tail sticking out and a broth poured into the center. Some of the food was to be eaten by your fingers, such as "ugali," a paste or porridge type substance that you mash with your fingers and drop into your mouth. I marveled at the simplicity of everything around me. It felt so much more alive, personal, and endearing.

I did my best to take in all the sights, sounds, smells, and culture as I sat quietly both listening to the conversation and talking amongst those around me as we awaited the arrival of our food. There was no radio, no television, no sounds outside of the immediate reality that we were living. Such a stark contrast to the constant diversions and distractions that we live daily. It felt good to be so present **in the moment**, fully engaged, rather than just be present in the body but absent in the mind.

We had been waiting for our food for about an hour or more when suddenly and without warning, the lights went out. Total darkness surrounded us. No other source of light but the moon. There we sat in the midst of a blackout, yet the conversation never missed a beat.

It was almost surreal. It felt amazing to see how quickly we all just adapted and overcame the sudden change of circumstances without stress or confusion.

It was so peaceful as Danielle provided her headlamp for light as it hung on a window. Others of us used the lighting from cell phones placed against, or below, water glasses to create a rippling lamp effect. It was an absolutely stunning affect that changed the already family filled, wholesome presence to an overall ambiance that emanated serenity.

The inviting sounds of voices, laughter, and light-hearted talk filled the void of the dark bouncing off the concrete walls and seemed to fill the room like a warm blanket.

Somewhere around two hours after we placed our request for food, the plates began coming to the table. I really didn't know what I was ordering but when it arrived, I smiled to myself and made a mental note of all the onions on my plate.

"Ok God, you're funny," was the thought running through my mind.

With a heart focused toward trusting Jesus, I ate the onions and waited for my body to begin violently rejecting the food that I just took in, but it was a reaction that ultimately never came. Forty-five years of an allergy and now…nothing. After dinner, we made our way back up to our rooms to shower and get some sleep before we resumed our journey to Songea, Tanzania the following day.

The Creep of Religiosity

It was decision time. My stomach was full, my room was prepared, but now was faced with the window to the world in my shower. I pushed back the cloth to get a better view of what was just outside my shower window that would not close. I was met with two smiling male faces that were all too quick to wave at me. I stepped back from the window toward the shower head, dropping the cloth back into place.

As I stood in my bathroom sizing up the task at hand, a decision had to be made. Option one…suck it up, straddle the toilet while taking a cold shower and displaying my nonchalance about my nudity as I wave at the people at the gas station next door or option two…walk over to my partner's room to determine if his room has better options and risk any pastoral judgments from members of the team.

I had to try. I turned the water on in the shower and went to close the bathroom door. Again, as I went to close the door behind me to shower, I stopped cold. Again, something in my spirit told me to not close the door to the bathroom which made no sense.

"What is going on?"

I turned off the water and returned to my bed. Regardless of what anyone might think or feel, I needed to make a decision based on my safety and well-being. I had to make a decision based on either religious concerns or trust in faith filled coverage.

After a few moments of sitting on my bed, I made the decision. I chose to explore the safety of Doyle's room for my shower. If anyone had an issue with that it was between them and God. Their issue was not with me.

I quietly walked past several of my team members' rooms, recalling my warning dreams and any Religious spirits I may encounter. I knocked on his door and asked to use his shower.

"Is everything ok?" he asked as he waved me into the room.

"Well, I have no hot water, I have no physical coverage, and my window doesn't close. I'm totally exposed."

Doyle being the gentleman that he is offered for me to check out his to see if it was any better.

With clothing in hand, I walked into his bathroom with the memories of the warnings about team members in my head.

"Well, this should add to any future judgment I might receive," I thought to myself. But I had to remember God was my guide, not religious driven concern. I just shook my head at the clear position I was intentionally being placed in. I was well aware that God is fully in control at all times and in all circumstances. Nothing is bigger than God and nothing is unknown to God. Therefore, God knew this quandary was occurring as well, and that also means God already has the purpose and outcome handled as well.

The reality was as much of the fleshly concerns that I had chosen to leave behind in my years on this earth, I still had the fear of what others might think plaguing me. Sadly, this was a preview and revelation of what was to be used against me on this trip. I just didn't consider how quickly Satan would jump into the mix.

As I took my shower, I looked up, grateful for the fact that there was hot water, but also for the fact that the window was up high, his toilet was slightly separated from the shower, and I could shut the door. Once I was finished in the shower, I realized

I had another issue, to walk through the hall in my pajamas and again risk judgment or put on those dirty clothes full of dust and travel grossness from all the places I had been that day.

Since I didn't know where the next location was or what our accommodations might be, I was unsure when I would be able to shower next. So, I opted for the clean pajamas while that option was still on the table.

As I dried off, with no place to sit, trying diligently not to fall on the wet glass tiled floor, I found myself laughing out loud. Loud enough that my partner asked me through the door, "Are you ok?"

I quickly assured him I was ok, but his response was equally as funny. "Uh, I hesitate to ask, but what's so funny?" I could hear the concern and confusion in his voice.

I envisioned what he must be hearing through the door. I laughed harder because what he must have been hearing had no real meaning to him without experiencing the dilemma I was in. I explained to him through the door and through laughter that I couldn't get dressed without getting all my dry clothing wet, but I couldn't come out and get dressed because he was there. I laughed at the thought of asking him to step into the bathroom while we switched places long enough for me to dress, but that just seemed ludicrous.

It was the equivalent of getting dressed inside of a porcelain bathtub, with no grips or texture on the bathtub surface and with no place to sit down or lean on. It was as if the Lord kept reminding me of the irony, "Don't forget you only have one fully functioning arm." But at least I wasn't straddling the toilet to shower. Everything was wet, slippery, and in the moment, extremely funny.

Once dressed, I needed to walk back to my room, barefoot, in my PJ's, with sopping wet hair, and no idea how to do it sneakily, and I didn't want to be sneaky. God knew what He was doing, so I opened the door, walked with my hair in a towel, my head held high, and a confident stride to my room. On the way over to my room, I passed a door. It was from that doorway I heard one of my team members casually say, "Hi." I backed up and looked her square in her face with love, waiting for the judgement to come. To my surprise, the judgement was not there.

"Hmmm, if it's not her, then who?" I wondered to myself.

After a quick exchange of hellos, I continued to my room and turned the key to lock myself in for the night. Crawling in bed, I wondered to myself, "What is around the corner that I'm being warned about?"

We were scheduled to leave at 6:00 a.m. for the seven-hour drive from Mbeya (where we stayed the night) to Songea. However, we were advised for safety reasons that we needed to alter our departure time to avoid some sort of conflict.

Rolling over for the night, I pulled the sheet up over me and fell quickly into sleep.

That morning I woke early to eat so we could begin our drive. I got up about 4:30 a.m. to repack and make sure my suitcase was locked and secured. Since I was up so early, I took the time to look at the world from the eyes of a local. It was breathtaking. Being blessed with the experience of watching the sun rise over Africa was something that cannot be explained. It was surreal.

My stomach began to growl and not willing to unpack my bag to get to the snacks I had brought with me, I walked down the narrow, unlit, uneven stairwell alone. Forgetting about how uneven it was, I missed the final step going down much farther and much faster than I had anticipated in my somewhat sleepy state. You can bet that when missing that last step occurred, by the time I landed, I was no longer in a sleep-soaked mind. I was wide awake.

Rounding a corner, I noticed another team member. We said good morning as he and I walked into the area we were dining in the night before. We began to talk between the two of us and announced, "Good morning," into the emptiness of the room hoping someone would hear us. Without any sound, up popped a head from behind the bar.

"Oh!" I said with a startled voice. "Good morning."

I wasn't prepared for anyone or anything thing to pop out of the bar but quickly came to understand that the staff slept on the floor of the restaurant behind the bar. As their guests, we were their top priority. As a result, they slept on the floor just to make sure they were there for us and prepared for us. No mattress, no pillow, just a concrete floor and a blanket.

The young man, still trying to blink the sleep out of his eyes, asked what we wanted for breakfast. As we began to tell him what we would like to have, he casually reached down and picked up his blanket. It was as if he was trying to get his bearings and determine if they had what we were asking for as he absently folded his blanket and set it to the side. This was apparently a normal way of doing business.

He was apologetically quick to say that they did not have most of what we asked for. We accepted his statement and asked what they did have. He gave us three options. We agreed and he nodded his head and disappeared to prepare the food.

One by one, people made their way down for breakfast and the room again became filled with laughter and banter. It was during breakfast that I heard the answer and explanation to one of my questions. Ashby, the lead evangelist on the trip, was telling the story of what occurred the evening before.

"I closed the bathroom door behind me, but it wouldn't let me back out." Ashby explained. "I was pounding on the door and yelling for someone to let me out."

We were all laughing at his account of what occurred and his embarrassment of another man on the team having to force the door open and set him free. Someone else indicated that their door also stuck, but they were able to jar it loose on their own.

Now the "don't close your door" message I received in my spirit made totally sense. I would have been trapped. After hearing Ashby's account of what occurred, the only thing that came to my mind was, "Thank you Jesus," and a sigh of relief.

Breakfast was uneventful but continued to be entertaining, as I watched suitcase and bag after bag being hauled down the narrow uneven staircase. These suitcases had seen many places over the years, but I couldn't help but laugh when I recalled the size of the suitcases of our team and the small statures of these sweet people that were hauling them up and down these steps. Doyle, being the gentleman that he is, grabbed the suitcase that I could not carry and got it set up in the loading area with all the other bags that started piling up. Jumping into the vehicles as they lined up to take us, we began the next leg of the journey.

Simple but Not Easy

It was so early but the world started bustling all around us. There was much to take in during the drive. Children walking to school for miles in one direction with buckets in their hands or on their head was the norm. After school, instead of walking straight home, they simply hike to the next location to find water in local streams or other places before walking several miles back home to begin their evening chores.

I recall thinking how bizarre it was to see such young children walking unsupervised for such distances with nothing but huts and grassland in between destinations. Children as young as six or seven make the trek to and from without question or complaint.

When Kingdoms Collide

In many ways, once they leave their village population, they are very much on their own. Witch doctors plague the area and prey on those who are "in need," as well as lost or innocent. Women and children walk or wander in these remote areas and are easy prey to the influences of Voodoo and Witch doctors. Witch doctors are regarded as credible medical options when someone is ill or injured. I learned that many people have a greater loyalty to the local Witch doctor than the clinics because the Witch doctors typically speak in a way that the villagers understand. The medical facilities speak in ways that do not inform but often intimidate or confuse. However, the Witch doctors speak without sterile medical terminologies and live within the communities or closer to the villages than outside medicine.

Witch doctors barter for most of their "business," while clinics were known to stay focused on agreed upon price, often more than the patient has. People walk far distances to get to the small cities where the clinics are and rarely have the ability to return due to their illnesses or impairments, leaving them stranded in places, often to die alone and virtually unknown.

In the marketplaces, I was mesmerized as I watched people lay rice onto tarps to dry, only to also watch the chickens wander over to the same tarps to eat their share. People did the same and nothing was strange about it. In the United States, such an act would get an entire distribution center shut down. But here, it is just an average day.

When Kingdoms Collide

Above: Tarp of rice drying as people walk through.

Next to those same type of tarps, men and women sit for hours picking rocks out of rice that were either brought in with the crop or that had been deposited by the chickens, livestock, or the shoes of people.

Women sit at tables in front of huts, cutting and peeling fruit for hours on end, so proficiently that they don't even look at what is in their hands. They cut the fruit by feel as they look around and converse with others doing the same. This was "real" life. Life uninterrupted by technology. It felt pure and sweet, even when we knew that what we were journeying toward was not going to be an easy mission.

As we got closer to Songea, the driver pulled over to the side of the road into an area where there didn't seem to be anyone around. Suddenly a black SUV pulled up. We were told nothing, and something was about to occur. I turned to those in the vehicle with us, "Are we part of some precession?" I asked. No one in our vehicle had any answers. Suddenly it became clear, we were being escorted into the city of Songea, but Doyle and I just were not expecting the reception the team received.

As we followed the SUV on the paved roads and approached the city of Songea, we were joined by more and more vehicles until we came to a stop. Suddenly, our vehicle was swarmed with people on all sides of us. It was confirmed, not by words since no one in our vehicle knew what was going on, but it was confirmed by the atmosphere. We concluded we were being met with a parade waiting for our arrival to begin, but that conclusion was incorrect. We WERE the parade. We began hearing the broken English words we could decipher over the loud speakers, like "Americans" and "Welcome."

Yep, it was clear, we WERE indeed the parade. A literal parade that was designed to welcome and announce our presence to the entire area of Songea. With our arrival, we brought the festival and teachings of Jesus to the people of Songea. We were photographed by people as they surrounded our vehicles, leaning into the cars, and holding out their hands to touch us.

As we slowly began the procession into the streets, hundreds more people lined the streets, waving with smiles that would light up a room. They leaned and twisted their bodies to look around others just to see into the windows of our transport vehicles.

Our procession wound up and down, in and out of the dirt "roads," as we began accepting our position and waving to and responding to the waves and smiles of people in every direction. Children were just wanting us to touch their hands, their heads, and their faces. As we leaned out of vehicles, people grabbed ahold and with their enthusiasm tried to pull some of us from the vehicles. Motorcycles did tricks and revved their engines in performances to show their excitement of our arrival. People waved branches, raising their voices in salute to our arrival. A sound truck, full of thumping music met us at the festival grounds to begin the formal announcements.

As we pulled to a stop, we remained in our vehicles not knowing how to navigate such a growing crowd without a translator. Ashby, the lead Evangelist who has been to Africa many times and had a translator, got out of the vehicle and began to welcome the people of Songea to the festival grounds. He began to whip up the ever-growing crowd with anticipation and pump them up for the event that was to come.

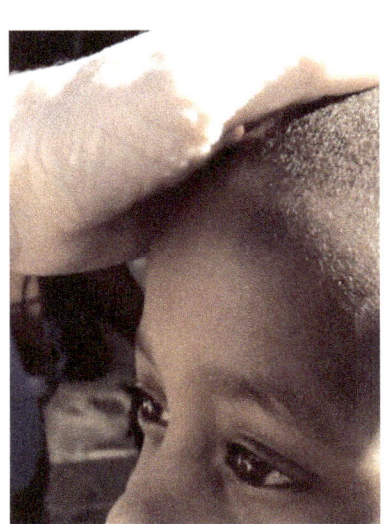 

This was a split population. There were Christian churches. However, those churches were overwhelmed and largely under taught. The remainder, and rather large part of the population, was Muslim or some other small sect of belief.

More and more people flooded the area, each looking for what was promised, conversations and teachings of Jesus. The craving was on their faces, and I instantly fell in love with every man, woman, and child I saw. These people were responding to the calling of the Holy Spirit, and they didn't even know it. What they did know was that the teachings of Jesus were in town, and it came with hope.

Person after person came up to our vehicles as they arrived taking pictures of us, the Americans that came to teach them about "this Jesus." Children came to our car doors, reaching up to us, reaching for our hands and arms as we watched all the interaction. People crowded around our vehicles in large numbers, some taking pictures and others just trying to get close.

Apparently, this was a much bigger deal then I was aware of. There was photo after photo, shaking hands with one person after another, grabbing at my clothing and touching my hair. Never had I considered that they had not seen a white lady with greying red hair before. So, my hair was apparently something to be petted.

The Chairman of Songea greeted us and shook our hands. Other governmental officials followed suit and motioned for us to have our photos taken with them. There was so much activity that no matter which direction I looked, someone was reaching, pulling, or talking to us.

After all the hubbub, we exited the area and proceeded to our bungalows in which we would be staying for the next ten days. I looked back to see people chasing us and waving at the departing vehicles. I couldn't understand the depth of their longing, and it wouldn't become clear until the following days when Doyle and I were on the streets. Alone, without our team.

It Becomes Personal

The first night in my assigned bungalow I slept amazingly well. It might have been even too well, because it was that night I received another a dream about what was to come. A dream that would be the rest of the warning that began before we left America. In the dream, my sweet team member Danielle was at a gas station like a truck stop. She needed gasoline for her vehicle. The gas station attendant asked her for her "I.D." Danielle reached into her purse and provided the attendant with a visual of her identification. In the dream, it was her driver's license that she was using. The attendant asked her to place it in his hand. However, in giving her license to the attendant, she was surrendering it to the authority of another. In that moment there was an exchange. When the attendant took her I.D., he handed her something with his other hand.

Danielle opened her hand and received what he was trading her I.D. for. It was a ring. A ring from a gas station, given to her by an unknown attendant that took her identification. Once she had the ring, she walked away from the vehicle because it either no longer worked or she no longer needed or wanted it.

As abruptly as that dream ended, another began. In that dream, Danielle and another woman, that would later be referred to as Jezebel on our team, decided to reach out for me. They felt the need to lay hands on me but there was no discernable reason except they felt compelled to. It was as if they were operating out of a compulsion that was almost robotic. Their eyes were no longer the eyes of someone I knew. Jezebel sat with her arms crossed with a deadened stare that never blinked. It was as if she believed she was in a power position and overtly puffed up her chest to display her belief.

Jezebel had a plan and Danielle was her pawn. In the dream, Jezebel's plan was to eliminate the seer and the prophetic. This was a spirit of pride and jealousy, and it was running hot and unchecked.

Soon, it became very clear in the dream that Jezebel was not going to stop at trying to take the gifts that God provided, but she wanted the competition and anyone who might expose her neutralized. Jezebel needed to be top dog and she needed to be above everyone else.

The dream continued as Jezebel instructed Danielle to pray for me. I held up my hands and informed them that I did not want prayer from them. Jezebel then twisted my words, "What? You're too good for prayer? That's pride. Don't worry, we will pray for that too."

I took a step back to avoid their touch, but Danielle leaned forward and began laying hands and praying for me against my wishes. I'll never forget the visual in the dream as Danielle's touch began pulling on my spirit. She was sucking the life right out of me. Her hands were acting as spiritual vacuums taking life from me at a steady rate, albeit little by little. I recall that I was actively bending backwards while she prayed to create distance and resistance. I remember looking in Danielle's eyes in the dream wondering, "Why would you do this to me? How can you be so deceived by this woman?"

Jezebel was calling the shots, but Danielle was following the plan. I recall asking the Lord to let me fight, but the Lord replied, "It's not your fight to have."

I felt betrayed by my friend who was so blindly following something so clearly influenced by evil. I recall forcefully telling

Danielle, "No!" and demanding that she snap out of it. "She's not who you think she is. You keep being deceived by this woman. Get away from her or get away from me."

It was as if she had gone deaf to the sound of my voice as she continued to suck the life out of me. I was far too exhausted to say anything further. It felt like my lungs were being vacuumed of all the air inside of them. My voice was gone, and my lungs were collapsed. Danielle was satisfied and Jezebel was smiling.

When I woke, I recognized the significance of this warning. I understood. It was about to hit the fan and I was in the crosshairs of a demonic woman. As has been our protocol for years, when I have such as significant dream or warning, I pick up the phone and notify Doyle immediately. He wasn't surprised at the dream. However, how this was all going to occur was unknown, and just who these other women were was yet to be determined. I had my suspicions, but they were only that…suspicions.

I just needed to be aware and take the warning to heart. The key in these circumstances is to know and acknowledge that God has <u>seen</u> it, God has shown me to let me know it's coming, and God <u>will do the work and protect me</u>. He said it's not my fight so I can only assume it's His, and I'm not going to get in the middle of whatever He was about to do.

Jezebel (whoever that might be) had chosen to partner with something that was not godly and in doing so, she had put the entire team at risk and chose to attack an upright woman of God.

Job 4:7-9

⁷ *"Consider now: Who, being innocent, has ever Perished?*
Where were the upright ever destroyed?
⁸ *As I have observed, those who plow evil*
And those who sow trouble reap it.
⁹ *At the breath of God they perish;*
at the blast of his anger they are no more

The next morning (Saturday), Doyle and I met for breakfast and entered into our morning prayers. I told Doyle about the dreams. He knew and trusted me enough to know that the warning was to be heeded, but nothing was going to stop us from our assignments.

With the unknown before us, experience propelling us, and faith uplifting us, we left behind the flesh and entered totally into the spiritual, praying out our unity and trust that God was going to move our feet according to His Will. We asked for coverage of each member of the team that was truly there for the people and for the Jezebel to be exposed. We asked for the team to have wisdom and discernment to see through the deception ahead of us and for unity to remain in the face of combat. Doyle's face was marked with concern for my safety. He knew something was coming for me, but neither of us would be deterred.

"Are you going to tell her?" Doyle asked when referring to Danielle and the dream.

"I don't feel like it is the right time," was my response.

I wanted to stay on my assignment and reject focusing on the looming attack. The warning was to help me understand and grow in my relationship and trust with God. Anything less would have been fruitless, counterproductive, and crippling in connecting with my spiritual flow.

"Shall we pray against it?" Doyle asked.

"No." It was clear that something needed to occur. It was clear that it would have to involve me, but God was doing something much bigger than what I could comprehend. I was going to be a pawn, and I settled into that understanding. Not only was I ok with that, but I found comfort in it. You see...God knows He can trust me to willingly step into the furnace and know that He is there. He doesn't have to trick me, test me, or throw me in kicking and screaming. Where He sends me, I will go. I was not going to get in God's way.

Once my ministry partner and I were ready, we sat patiently waiting in the lobby for the mystery car of the day to arrive with the mystery driver that would take us to an unknown location. This alone was an exercise in faith. We were the first of this type of team that was to do such a thing as be dropped into the villages. So, we had no idea what we're walking into or what it was like. The unknown awaited.

When the mystery vehicle arrived, we jumped in, trusted we had the right vehicle and got out when told. It really was that simple. With no interpreter and no experience at speaking Swahili, we were just wading through every experience with nothing more than our smiles and our faith. We drove and drove, and with each mile I wondered just how far we would be from the team. We had no cell service to access anyone. It was just Doyle and I looking out the windows and enjoying the weirdness that we were living.

Finally, the vehicle pulled up to a building and came to a stop. We looked at him as he worked to convey to us that this was a church and we needed to get out. Looking around, I laughed out loud. There was no one around. No pastor, no villagers, and more importantly, no interpreters.

The driver motioned for us to get out of the vehicle, so we grabbed our things and opened the car doors. It was then that we heard such a racket it was hard to decipher. It sounded like music, chanting, a public announcement, and instruments all at the loudest volume possible.

We were no more than a few steps from the vehicle when it took off and left us standing alone in the middle of what felt like nowhere, but we headed toward the sound. It was then that our appearance was noticed, and men came from every direction. The men were all speaking at once and all motioning in the same direction, but it wasn't into the church they were taking us. They were taking us someplace BEHIND the church. None of these men spoke English and it became clear that none of these men were our interpreters. Doyle took my hand and held a firm grip on it as we were asked to continue walking past the church. Whatever was going to occur, we were in it together.

We stopped in front of an extremely small building that was barely big enough for a small desk and two chairs. It was less like a building and more like a room. They motioned for me to sit in one of the chairs. I let go of Doyle's hand so I could turn around and sit. As I did so, I ascertained my surroundings. There was nothing on the desk, nothing on the walls, and nothing in this room other than the desk and chairs. What was this place? It was so small that not all the men could fit into the room.

The men were chattering away looking at Doyle. At some point, I heard broken English come from one of the men and then another. "Yes!" I thought to myself. We have an interpreter, or at least I was hoping.

I sat quietly, surrounded by six men. Doyle was working to bridge the gap between the men. Several motioned toward me. However, Doyle reached forward and took my hand to send the message that we were a team. In those moments, if fear was allowed to creep in even the slightest, panic would have ruled that entire scene. It felt like the perfect beginning of any action movie in which Americans are abducted or beaten and robbed to be left for dead. Now please don't think I'm just being dramatic.

This area is known for its kidnappings as you will see in later pages.

The music of the adjacent church celebration was blasting all around us. The men were yelling over the sound so that they could be heard. It felt like we were trying to have a conversation in the center of a rock concert. Ironically, as I listened to all the yelling in this confined space, there was total peace inside me. It took some time but ultimately, we learned that these men were Pastors.

They were trying to understand what our needs were so they might best accommodate us. In this understanding, Doyle released his grip on me and took the other open seat in this small room. He began expressing what it was that we were there to do and what we were going to need to make it happen. The men all leaned in as closely as possible to hear what they could from us. The men looked over at me. However, in accordance with their culture and respectful roles, I motioned for Doyle to continue to speak on my behalf.

As it turned out, the men wanted to split up Doyle and I and move according to a formula that they thought would be best based on their knowledge of how church was to be taught to the people. What they didn't understand, and truly they did not, we were going to move according to the unctions of the Lord Himself, not according to their earthly knowledge. We knew we were to remain together for the best outcome of the people. If two by two was good enough for God to send people in the Bible, then it was good enough for us. We didn't need to explain any further. We would not be divided. We entered into this journey as a pre-ordained partnership, and we will end this journey as a unified partnership. We took our stand, our mission, and our partnership will not be divided nor watered down.

Doyle looked at the faces that kept pressing forward to hear, "We flow according to the spirit. All we need is to get where we are going. Where the people are that we need to talk to."

They seemed perplexed. Doyle found himself explaining what it meant to flow in the spirit, and I smiled as the interpreters struggled to convey that information to the Pastors. It was as if it was such a foreign concept, and it was not something that they wished to explore. Again, they tried to separate us as they began to take our belongings from me.

They attempted to remove everything we were carrying, including my purse (which only held emergency food, emergency battery pack for my phone, and secondary I.D.), our water supply, and my phone. I quickly retrieved my phone. One of the men held out his hand to take it from me and I shook my head "no." This is one belonging I held my ground on. "I'm sorry, but no. I will keep this with me. I want to take pictures." With that, he seemed to accept the answer as a reasonable one and lowered his hand. Another man took my partner's backpack, his Bible, and the flyers we carried for the festival.

This action caught us completely off guard because no one asked or said a word. Everything was just kind of "taken." Not sensing any aggression or danger, we didn't' resist but simply expressed to them that we were "used to carrying our own stuff." It was only then it was explained to us that guests were never to labor, that guests were not to carry anything, and the hosts were to carry everything. What?! This loving hospitality was something I've never experienced.

I could not help but smile as I watched my male interpreter put my purse strap over his head and shoulder and carry it for hours, unapologetically, and unembarrassed. I was going to bring a backpack instead of a purse but in the last moments of packing, decided not to put any unnecessary pressure on the injured shoulder. This meant the backpack was out…and the purse was in.

After all the dickering, we got back into a vehicle with yet another driver and waited to see what was next. One of the men in the small room warned us that the Muslims had bad attitudes toward Christians, and we needed to be careful. Taking that into consideration, we settled in for another ten-minute ride to another unknown area. Before getting out, we were advised in broken English, "This is where Muslims. They live here." With a nod of understanding, Doyle and I were dropped off with nothing more than our interpreters, our personalities, and our love of Jesus to protect us.

Regardless of what we may be taught or how Muslims might be portrayed, not all Muslims are angry or encourage violence, but there are some that are clear that they will not tolerate Christians teaching about King Jesus on their turf. We were warned, but we were not concerned. This was our journey, but it's the Father's plan.

Indeed, we did find ourselves in situations that we were advised were unsafe while we were on the streets, but we did not feel deterred. We pushed further into their territory, confident that our Lord would handle anything we encountered with love.

My personal interpreter continued with his warnings in his broken English, "We are walking into places that we are not welcome in. We must be wise."

Inside of me, I felt the Holy Spirit ignite in response to the words. "This is where I love to be," was my response. My interpreter continued to try and emphasize his concern and caution. However, Doyle and I assured him we were very comfortable in moving forward. Looking back, I'm not sure if he was concerned about us or them. Either way, fear would not be permitted as a deterrent.

Americanized Thinking

Once out of the vehicle and into what many would consider as enemy territory, without notice, my interpreter took me by my hand and began to lead me through the streets as if he had known me forever. I shot Doyle a look and to my surprise, he just smiled as he watched from a few feet behind us. From an American perspective, it was quite a scene. Two people who don't know each other, walking hand in hand, talking and swinging our hands like a couple of children.

The immediate acceptance of each other was uncanny. Two people from separate continents, opposite genders, different cultures, completely different skin tones, yet the loving acceptance superseded everything. There was no fear of illness we might bring from another continent or even during our travels through Africa, even while there was another Ebola outbreak in other parts of Africa during that time. They lived day to day.

I couldn't help but reflect on all the division that exists in America. Race, economic status, political positions, popularity status and in the year 2020, the Covid-19 divide entered into the ever divisive cauldron to be stirred. In America, we may be the most progressive country under God, but these people were the most loving and Christ-like I've ever experienced on earth. We were not strangers. These men were my brothers, and I was their sister. My interpreter began to hum a song as we continued to walk hand in hand through the dirt roads of a village full of enemy fire.

Cultural Note: Over the next few days, I observed local men holding the hands of other local men, men holding the hands of local women, and local women with local women. These wonderful people were more civilized than most people I know, because they were unashamed of the open love that they shared for each other. Unapologetic love. They had discovered something that I've known all my life. The same thing that I have been criticized about all my life. The same thing that Jesus tried to teach...human connection and true relationship.

They understand the value of connection, the value of sharing, and the value of kind gestures. Here, we relegate touch to a diminished value of a sexual context, thereby robbing each other of the love that we are supposed to have for each other.

One of the handshakes that African's have is that of honor. They place the left hand on the arm of the right hand, as they take the right hand of the person they are showing honor to. Other times, women take you by the hand or hands, look you directly in the eyes, curtsy and drop their eyes in honor. Hand holding seemed to convey trust, like-mindedness, unity, and acceptance.

Can you imagine if people here could adopt this same understanding? I pray that we, here in the United States, can regain the sweetness and innocence lost in such a simple connection, but sadly, I believe that Jesus will have to come first. This was an amazing display of living in connection and relationship. In many ways, I experienced such an exchange. The exchange of my teaching the locals about Holy Spirit and the locals teaching me about honor and the depths of humility that I've never seen.

Choosing "The Way" vs. Living by "The Rules"

Street Evangelism Day #1

We stumbled upon several young men. They were fixing or working on various motorcycles and mechanisms that they were building. I refer to them as mechanisms because these wonderful people turn so many things that we consider trash into usable and time saving gems for daily living.

Apparently, this was where we were going to get our feet wet in creating and establishing ourselves in the area. Both spiritually, as well as physically. You see...word travels quickly in both realms and it was about to become obvious. Initially, I stood quietly as all these men began to talk. I was taking my time in tapping into the spirit and getting a feel for the land. I needed to know from the Lord how were to proceed. Human direction had its value, but Kingdom input is invaluable.

Surveying the men, I scanned from side to side looking at each one. Repeatedly, the one in the red shirt jumped out to both me, as well as Doyle. All of them made sure that they kept their distance. However, we had our assessment, so Doyle and I stepped forward. Our interpreters followed our cues as they learned us. We asked him if he knew about Jesus.

He smiled and stated, "I'm a Muslim," but continued to express an interested in hearing about "this Jesus."

He was kind but very guarded and his face was as hard as marble. He was clearly taking a risk in speaking to us, constantly looking over his shoulder at the other Muslim men who were standing and sitting all around. More began to gather as we were noticed by the villagers.

Ignoring the growing level of interest that was forming around Doyle and I, we continued to tell the man in red about the "Good News." We began to tell him of the love of Jesus. We explained to him about the cross and the life Jesus gave up so he could have a life of freedom, knowing that Jesus rose and Holy Spirit came, so that he may have eternal life in Heaven and a connection to the Holy Father while still on this earth.

He was intent on his listening to what was being said. Something was ringing in his spirit as true as he became less and less concerned about the other Muslims that were beginning to press forward in an unknown agenda. These men began drifting forward. We saw them moving in on us, but it didn't matter to Doyle and me because as we spoke, we watched a visible change in the man's facial expressions. He was suddenly softer, intent on hearing what we had to say, instead of being intense. We were witnessing Holy Spirit supernaturally touch a young man. A man who spoke no English, trusting total strangers with receiving "truth." It was a truth that the young man could not explain with words, but his spirit knew the truth when it heard it. He expressed through our interpreters that he felt something inside of him that felt weird but good. He was receiving.

Doyle, I, and the man in red knew God was breaking some type of socially acceptable rules in talking to us. The lurking men were beginning to make it clear with their sneers and talking louder over our prayers, but the man in red was following what he knew was right.

After speaking and praying for him, I gave him a Word I felt was from the Lord. As I delivered it, he almost began to cry. His eyes teared as He felt the depth of the word.

We asked, "Would you like to receive Jesus as your Lord and Savior?" His reply was thoughtful and carefully considered. We gave him a moment of silence before we asked a different way, "Would you like to receive Jesus into your heart?"

This time his response was clear as he looked at me and then Doyle. His eyes shifted just past Doyle. The man in red saw the others watching with arms crossed and talking. They never took their eyes off us and the man in red. I was impressed with the strength and conviction this man had to follow his heart and the call in his spirit in the face of so much adversity. His reply was soft but clearly stated, "Yes, I want this Jesus."

Doyle took his hands and led him to Jesus. However, before we left, the man in red surveyed the people that gathered around him and by proximity Doyle and I as well. He requested one more thing. He looked us in the eye and spoke the reality that he faced, "I need prayer of protection." As the man in red said the words, more people gathered with audible agitation increasing as witnesses to him accepting this foreign God…Jesus.

Doyle and I glanced around again, taking a visible inventory of what was occurring. Acknowledging the danger that was looming, we both assured him that God is greater than all of what he was seeing. As Doyle spoke to him through the translator, I turned around and let it be known that I knew their intent and let my body language convey that there would be no fear here and instead love would be conveyed. Love is actually far more powerful than anything else on this earth.

I turned backed to Doyle and the man in red as we proceeded to audibly take authority praying the protection of the blood of Jesus over this young man and our journey in this foreign land.

We witnessed the flood of relief that covered his face as we assured him that God watches over His children and that he was one of God's children.

As Doyle and I began to walk away, we were halfway across what would be considered a commercialized salvage yard here in America, when another young man called out to us from a distance. We asked our interpreter what was going on. He advised us that another young man was irritated that we didn't pray for him.

Doyle and I exchanged glances. "How odd," I thought to myself. We were in Muslim villages, literally surrounded by agitated Muslim young men who were watching our every move. Yet this young man, in his mid-twenties, was feeling jilted for not getting the same opportunity to receive Jesus as the man in red.

Doyle and I smiled at what was going on. This young man was willing to face the glaring men in pursuit of something that was calling on his heart and spirit. Open intimidation was around us, but peace was on us.

We walked back over into the lion's den without hesitation. The young man that was yelling stood at a higher elevation than the young man in red that we had just prayed for, so we never saw him. I looked up and surveyed the area above us that I had not seen before, and this young man was the only one there. Where did he come from?

Noting his arms crossed and the scowl on his face, we asked him through our interpreters what he needed. He advised us his name was Lucas. He openly announced from where he was standing that he was a Muslim, but his wife was Christian, and he wanted to accept Jesus. Lucas was not even slightly trying to hide the fact that he was clearly angry with us for not praying for him earlier. Instead of entertaining the agitation he was expressing and the demand he was making, we told him we needed to ask him a few questions.

Once we began talking to him about the life, death, resurrection, and forgiveness of Jesus, his face began to soften. It was always such a strange sensation to have experienced such peace while surrounded by such hostility. Lucas' eyes no longer had a look of confrontation. Instead, it was of interest and a desire to understand. Lucas began to ask questions about Jesus. He truly wanted to understand. He continued to flood us with questions until there was a long silence, only for that silence to be shattered with the words, "I'm ready to accept Jesus as mine." While we talked to Lucas and he asked questions, the silence from the surrounding men was almost deafening.

As Lucas uttered the words asking for Jesus, Doyle and I looked at each other. Personally, I was assessing the man to confirm that he was understanding what he was requesting. But the moment Lucas raised his head and looked at me, I saw the smile in his eyes. In that moment, I knew he was ready. It was then that we administered the prayer of salvation and the men around us became vocal again. We listened intently as Lucas repeated the words from his heart, his hands in ours, and head down in reverence to the Jesus he was welcoming into his heart.

Upon the completion of this prayer, he raised his head with a smile that reached from ear to ear. His joy was clear and obvious. His face almost glowing while those around us disapproved at his choice.

Lucas began to explain that he had been wanting this but didn't know how to get Jesus inside him. He desired "this Jesus" but the path to Jesus was unclear and marred in religious hurdles that he could not leap. I've heard many things during my time in ministry, but the next question still brings tears to my eyes.

"May I ask you permission for something?" Lucas questioned.

I responded with, "What is it?"

"Can I got to church with my wife now?"

So there it was, a direct conflict…we were advised that we needed to heed and adhere to the culture in order to better ensure our safety while in Songea. However, in this moment we were faced with a question that was in conflict with the cultural environment…and we were outnumbered.

Lucas further explained he wanted more than anything to go to a Christian church with his wife, but it was forbidden because he was born and raised a Muslim. He said he didn't choose it, but the Muslim faith chose him.

Doyle, being so graceful and gentle, responded, "Pray about it." However, apparently, I needed to speak something more direct because out of my mouth and in breaking all the rules of social etiquette came the one simple truth, "If there is no law against it in your land, then yes, go to church with your wife. Marriage is a covenant and God would honor that covenant in church no matter what anyone says."

As soon as it was out of my mouth, I almost audibly gasped. The response caught me off guard as it left my mouth. My flesh wanted to apologize but my spirit said no. I accepted the fact that what came from me was not of me and therefore was of God, so

I chose to further explain, "As long as you don't risk yourself or your family beyond what you are willing to risk, you should go where God is calling you to."

Lucas reiterated that the desire of his heart was to go to church to learn about Jesus with his wife. Seeing his eyes convey the feeling he was experiencing, I further explained that what God says is far more valuable than what social acceptance dictates. To reinforce such a position, Doyle and I began to convey to him Romans 12:2 and the meaning behind it.

This same theme would rear its head several more times throughout this trip before we were to head back home. Lucas was so excited that he took us by our hands and showed us appreciation and love through his hand movements in mine. He looked over to the elevated area behind where he was standing. He explained that he was inside his hut when we approached but heard us. That explained why we did not see him before. He said he and his wife were sleeping upon our arrival, but he felt he had to get up and see us. Lucas smiled so big when he spoke his final statements to us. His smile deepened at this gesture and said, "She will be so happy. I thank you so much. I can be with my wife now."

The radiance that displayed on Lucas' face as he walked in the direction of his wife will be a look that I hope to always remember.

The looming, sneering and disapproving faces turned away from us when we turned to face them and proceeded down onto a dirt path that seemed to weave in and out.

These paths are not easy to describe. The methodology of the paths is to get from one place to another as efficiently as possible, which means they cut through all areas. Nothing was trespassing. One moment you may be walking through someone's chickens and the next through someone's garden. Other times, we found ourselves behind or between huts, not sure who or what was waiting when we were to emerge. Many of these paths have holes so large each could consume a vehicle without any issue or effort. Ironically, we would soon come to learn that this would be one of the easier roads to walk on for some time to come.

Ignition Point

As we walked down these dirt paths, we drew more and more attention to our presence. I could feel the eyes on me. A very white woman, wearing a clearly pronounced cross around her neck in a Muslim community. "Yep, that's smart," I mused to myself.

Here I was on a journey that felt so right. Every smile I had for someone was genuine and I unapologetically loved on everyone. It was if I was oblivious to the circumstances of the resentment around us. God was proving with every step of my foot that He was greater than the color barriers, the language barriers, the gender barriers, and the religious barriers that could have separated all of us.

We entered one portion of a Muslim village that was very spiritually dark. The people seemed to almost be moving in slow motion around me. Doyle and I had become somewhat separated. I could see him, and he could see me, but we were not close in proximity.

Suddenly without warning, my flesh said, "Danger! Turn around. Look!"

But the spirit said, "Go and flow. Daughter of God is covered."

Behind me and my interpreter, I was being watched and preyed upon. The devil was plotting against me, but God was overruling the plot, so relax is exactly what I did. I felt at peace, happy, and loved being where I "shouldn't" feel such a thing.

I turned and looked for my partner and saw that he was on the other side of the roadway talking with several children as dozens of people walked by. Each person eyeing me and carrying their goods for the day. It was then that I realized I had relaxed so much that I allowed my partner to be at a distance that most would say is unsafe for me and yet, I had peace.

I continued to keep moving forward hoping that Doyle would soon catch up. A woman wearing traditional Muslim attire walked up, careful to avoid my gaze. I could feel her part in the plan. She was sent to find out how to get to me. She refused to look at me as she spoke directly to my interpreter.

"Where are the American Christians staying?" she hissed as she slid me a look of disgust. She had decided to be clear in letting me know she had nefarious intentions.

My interpreter told her the name of the bungalow that I was staying in. I slid my interpreter a look when I recognized the name of where we were staying came out of his mouth as he continued to speak with the enemy's vessel. He saw me looking at him and stated, "Ma'am, I assure you, they cannot get in there."

The woman went on to ask him a few more questions while trying to hide a scowl and anger towards me. Questions like, "How long are they here?" and asking about our specific departure plans. After my interpreter answered her questions, I looked directly in her eyes and told her I loved her through my interpreter. She softened just a bit and said she loved me too. I watched as she quickly turned and moved at a fast pace to catch up with others that she had been with.

"Well, that wasn't subtle," I said to my interpreter.

"No, not at all," he responded.

Not sure what was going to transpire in the flesh, but I knew the calculated movements had already started in the spirit. In some ways it didn't matter because I trusted in God. However, in the spirit, I needed to remain armored up, and I knew just how to do that.

A short time later we, my interpreter and I, walked up on a Muslim family sitting in the area outside of their house. By this time, I had become comfortable being more or less on my own. I know that sounds crazy, but I was at home in the flesh and in the spirit. So why not?

Most of the people in Songea were outside of their homes or huts to stay cool or for light during the daytime hours. There is very little to no running water. Any running water they might have, came from hand pumps outside in common areas. The houses are crafted from mud made into handmade bricks that supported the roofs made from scrap metals, and dirt floors. Food consisted of whatever grows in the yard or whatever animals they are able to raise or catch. Chickens, roosters, and small animals walking around my feet and legs became a common occurrence, so much so I stopped noticing.

Upon walking up to this Muslim family, I noted that there were many of them. Some sitting on the ground, some sitting on logs, but all were collectively working in unity in preparing their meal for the day.

It was a truly charming scene. Children running around freely. Several women talking and working. While it was charming, it was also painfully quiet. There was not a lot of talking, or joy in their faces. Perhaps it was because the Christian Americans were there. However, the Holy Spirit was about to blow through there and change that. Doyle and I had no power to do what was to occur next, but God did.

The first young lady I walked up to was clearly struggling with the fact that there were Christians at her house. The struggle was almost written on her face. As her eyes bounced between me and her hands without raising her head, it was clear she wasn't sure if she should make eye contact, but also wasn't sure if she should avoid eye contact either. She couldn't hide her body language. She was nervous. It had gotten around the village that the Christian Americans were there, and they were bringing stories of a powerful God. News traveled fast. She continued with her task of sorting food and smiled as she continued to fidget.

It became clear as I approached that I needed to show her honor in her home. When I came to the clearing of her home so that we were just a few feet from each other, I spoke, "Habari!"

They responded the same, "Habari" but with far less enthusiasm. There was trepidation in their voices, but they were choosing to be hospitable. I turned to my interpreter with a decided humility to display to them I was not a threat. In doing so, I introduced myself and asked for their permission to speak. Through my interpreter, I began to speak to them about my Jesus.

After a few moments of contemplation in their eyes, they graciously motioned for me to sit as my translator squatted next to me. By this time, Doyle had caught up with me and my interpreter and began introducing himself.

My gaze swept over the reactions to Doyle's entry. A young lady looking to be in her early twenties appeared so sweet in her yellow scarf sitting off by herself under a tree. At first, she would barely look at either of us, diverting her eyes and avoiding my gaze by looking down at her hands. It was then that the Lord flooded a Word into my spirit, and it was meant for her. I slowly approached her. It was like walking up to a skittish child. My interpreter followed me and as I began to speak, he gave her the Word that the Lord had given.

"Habari," I spoke very softly. She returned the greeting with a smile and a whispered response of the same.

"Do you know why I'm here?" I asked.

She shook her head no.

"What a pretty scarf. It's beautiful on you," I said with all genuineness. She smiled, and what a smile. It was so amazing that it caught me off guard. "Can I tell you something I know about you?" I asked her through the interpreter.

She slowly shook her head yes.

"I know you are not feeling safe." She and I locked eyes. She and I both knew we were not talking about that specific moment, but that she didn't feel safe in her daily life. I had the feeling that she had been raped or in fear of that, so I felt compelled to continue.

"Jesus knows you don't feel safe here, in your life. Is that true?"

She turned her head away as far from me as possible.

I recognized her gaze in that moment. She was trying to mentally escape. I continued in the same soft tone. "Do you know who Jesus is?" I asked.

She replied with a nod of her head. Tears were running down her face. She couldn't contain the emotion that was overriding her abilities to subdue them.

"Jesus is the protector of your soul." The moment I said those words her head spun around to me. Her eyes were filled to the rim with tears that were just waiting to fall.

She turned her head away again, sitting quietly as I explained in more detail the love of Jesus and what that means for her life here on earth today. After a few minutes, she turned her face back in my direction. Gathering her composure, she looked down at her hands and spoke ever so quietly. "Mama...," she said with a long pause, "I want this Jesus." This quiet little young lady who would not even look me in the eyes, chose to honor me by calling me "Mother."

"Are you sure?" I inquired.

The interpreter spoke the answer that she just provided. "Yes, mama. I do want this Jesus."

I asked permission to hold her hands. It was then that I turned my head and noticed no less than ten other women and children standing there with a Muslim man. They became the witnesses to her decision. She slowly held out her hands, looked me in the eye and repeated after me. Word for word she repeated with eyes streaming with tears and a smile on her face. After some time of gaining her composure, she walked over and put her hand on my head to snap the photo of us.

I told her that I was proud of her and that I loved her. It was clear that she was touched deep in her spirit as she cried and smiled holding my hand and not wanting to let go.

As soon as I felt the moment was over, knowing that people had again crowded around us to hear what I was saying, I turned to them and surveyed their faces. They were close enough in proximity that there was no doubt in my mind that they had heard the story of Jesus as I spoke it to the lovely young lady in yellow. I turned around and asked the oldest woman if she would like to accept Jesus. I saw a strange mix of fear and a "yes" flash in her eyes, but her lips said no. Her inner conflict was apparent not only to me but to all others there. I respected what she said and turned to another woman offering her the "Prayer of Jesus." The woman in red (seen in the next photo) jumped at the chance and said that she wanted the freedom that Jesus offered.

Like a small child, this adult woman, giggled and smiled,

hardly containing her excitement. She was almost embarrassed at her excitement, becoming sheepish behind her smile like a grinning child hiding behind the legs of a parent wanting to see. I understood what she was feeling because the touch of the Holy Spirit was felt by all. The entire area was lit up in laughter. She quickly held out her hands as she had seen the young lady in yellow do and the anticipation was making her almost shake. I took hold of her hands and asked that she repeat after me in the prayer of salvation. All at once, it was as if a warm blanket wrapped around us, and she was washed with a calm serenity as she repeated the words. The words were soft but so very sincere. It was as if the words were coming from so deep that she could hardly express them. Every cell was in agreement with her words. As this was occurring, more and more children gathered around us. They watched and listened to the "Good News" of Jesus. The children's eyes danced at the stories of Jesus, often giggling, and bouncing around talking amongst themselves as children do. But without fail, they each came back for more stories.

I fought back tears as I watched children mouthing words of the prayer of Jesus as the translator spoke after me.

The woman in red busted out in laughter and joy the moment the word "Amen" was uttered. She could no longer contain herself and neither could the children.

We stayed and chatted a bit more just to let them know we were there for them. God was right there with us, enjoying His children. We could feel Him and so could they.

At that same location, my partner was speaking with an older man. I don't personally know his story, because I was involved with the other people, but I noticed he had fangs for teeth. I do recall that upon arrival, just like the others, he was expressionless, bordering on glum. But just like the others, after my partner led him to Jesus, he just could not stop giggling and laughing. The scene was almost too much to take in.

This solemn group of people, who were originally unwelcoming and disturbed at our walking into their Muslim home, were overwhelmed with a joy, laughter, and giddiness that broke all barriers. None could have planned the hugging, and the silliness that followed. Several of them chose to unburden themselves with confession. They were pleading forgiveness from Jesus for following something that was not Godly. They were finding peace and being so open about it. Nothing was hidden as they continued stating their frustrations and the harsh actions taken toward each other over the last several years. As they smiled and laughed, they were expressing their lack of hope that had permeated their lives, yet now they were overjoyed and filled with new life and hope.

"Thank you for bringing the hope Jesus to us. We don't deserve it, but we want it," one of the women said.

Looking her in the eyes, I responded, "None of us deserve it, but He offers hope freely to all of us."

"Please come back someday," they were all speaking over each other with invitations to join them again during this trip and future trips.

As we walked away, I turned around and spoke my heart, "I love you all," and I meant it.

This was something I wanted all of them to know, that they were loved, truly, deeply, and we were family. It was very special to watch them actually receive the words of love with the genuineness that I intended.

"Asante sana, asante sana, nakupenda!" which meant thank you and I love you.

"Nakupenda!"

"Nakupenda!"

Each person was yelling that simple word at our departing backs as we walked away.

We continued our journey on foot as we have been throughout this adventure. Children played everywhere, unsupervised, without adults. As a mother, I cringed when I considered the number of predators (animal, reptilian, human, and spiritual) that must be around while these children played. Children as young as 2 were wandering around from structure to structure, from cow or chicken to tree or street. They made toys out of what they might find in the dirt, and a game from anything they could climb or throw. Life here was so simple as I watched innocence flourish in every direction. Little boys in every village had a wadded-up cloth that they tossed around as a ball. They rolled old tires from vehicles everywhere they went as a continuous game and they climbed whatever was climbable, while little girls danced or hung out running from place to place.

In all of this, there was such an essence of trust, purity, and freedom in the midst of having nothing but the clothing on their backs. It was impossible not to laugh and play along with the children. I couldn't help but imagine life in America this way. I found myself saying, "Life should be this simple everywhere." It felt almost biblical, which was ironic because we were among Muslims who didn't know what that meant.

Axe Man Standoff

Still floating on that Holy Spirit filled moment, we continued our journey over to the next area of the village. There were a couple of women sitting in the dirt under a tree. They sat next to what we would learn to be clay stoves that they created to sell. They were waiting next to their creations for the clay to dry.

I was struck by the silence between the two women as well as the physical distance that they kept from each other. They seemed so sad, but I had no idea what was to come might actually explain some of that unhappiness.

When they saw us coming, again as others before, they averted their eyes and upon our approach they turned their heads away from us. Their demeanor was cold, but their eyes spoke something completely different. It was as if they were acting a predetermined part or expectation. The body language was established to express to us, "Go away," but their eyes kept drawing me in. There was fear in the air for these women, but where was the threat? Was it us? The American preachers? Was it the message of Jesus? The reality was they were responding to the anticipation of looming conflict.

Have you ever had that family member you know is going to cause trouble at a family gathering? The one family member that just looks for reasons to argue. The overprotective, the unstable, the overbearing family member that you just don't want to invite? We couldn't see him, but that was what the women were waiting for...he was lurking.

We learned that our team was the main topic of conversation all over Songea. The word of our presence in Songea spread quickly, so it was only a matter of time before it collided with us. Doyle and I glanced at each other. Silently, we knew we were walking into a trap of sorts. We were the target. Neither one of us would be deterred, so we moved forward. I approached the women while Doyle stood from a different vantage point. With total confidence in Doyle, I focused on the women.

"We've come to invite you to the festival and the teachings of the Good News of Jesus."

Doyle stepped forward and gave one of the women a small flyer with the festival information on it. One woman initially took it and looked at it. She lowered her head to read it, however her head remained down as she placed it back into the hand of the interpreter. She said it was against the Muslim rules to have something Christian in her hand. Understanding her dilemma, we took back the flyer and I focused on the love that she was missing.

There was the sound of aggression behind me. Turning, I saw Doyle and his interpreter addressing a man that had come out from behind a hut holding a very sharp-edged axe. Doyle had his hands up in front of him to show him we were unarmed. The women referred to the man with an axe as "Papa." It was clear that Papa saw us as a threat and his axe was the weapon of his choice.

Turning away from "Papa," I quickly addressed the women. I knew that Doyle could handle the angry "Papa," but I knew our time here was limited and wearing out fast. The interpreter sensed the same as he turned with me, and we knelt closely to the women. We needed to speak to them without Papa dictating the dialogue.

Trusting that Doyle literally had my back, I remained focused and totally engaged with these women. The woman in the yellow and red wrap, seen facing the camera in the shadows, said to me through my interpreter, "I've liked you since I saw you coming." To hear the words, see how genuine the words were, to watch the warmth of her smile, and the twinkle in her eyes, I found myself fighting in the spirit for her to find strength in the struggle. I could see her inner battle as she glanced from me to her "Papa." She spoke in hushed tones. I could feel her struggle.

"Papa" was holding his ground and protecting the women from this Christian God. His voice being projected over the conversation that Doyle was having as a purposeful distraction for me and what I was conveying to the women.

Papa was clear, "I don't want anything to do with this Jesus."

Just like all the others, Papa avoided all eye contact but kept his axe at the ready. He appeared vengeful and let us know we were not welcome there. Now I understood the depth of the struggle the women were dealing with. Their eyes conveyed "help" and "welcome," but Papa was overbearing, and they feared for either us, themselves, or perhaps both.

"We're never going to change!" said Papa as he moved his body awkwardly to make us feel as unwelcome as possible.

I glanced over at Doyle and saw a relaxed stance in his body language. I shifted my hearing to focus on my partner's voice. I heard Doyle's signature softness and lilt that he places into his voice to convey compassion and understanding. Papa seemed to be responding well to it. I felt no reason to respond to the threat regardless of the weapon in his hand or the anger Papa was expressing. Regardless of Papa, I was there for the women.

In response to the woman's statement that she liked me as soon as she saw me coming, I told the woman that I felt the same way and that I liked her from the time I met her. I continued to speak to her about Jesus as Doyle's focus remained focused on talking with "Papa."

I told her of the love of Jesus and if she wanted to learn more, more was available to learn. She looked over at Papa and obediently repeated, "We are Muslim." I smiled at her letting her know I understood.

"Is that what you want?" I probed.

She remained silent but her eyes held my gaze. I knew she was trapped, and we were on their turf, so I needed to be careful rather than set off the entire village. As softly as I could, I spoke, "Would you like me to pray for you?"

Just as softly, she replied in Swahili, "Yes."

After hearing that, I made sure she understood my question, "I pray in the name of Jesus. Are you ok with that?

She softly said, "Yes." She said that she wanted that.

I understood her request and she understood what I was saying. Before we departed, I quietly said, "You can pray in your head to Jesus if you want to. He can hear you even if you don't make sound."

She nodded as I stood up to leave.

With that movement, Doyle extended gratitude to Papa for allowing us to spend time with him and his family. It was then that Papa dropped the axe. We said your goodbyes and honored Papa with messages of thanks and being honored by Papa's presence. You see…even though the oppressive spirit was working to isolate these women, the seeds were planted. It's not our job to control the outcome. Our duty is to spread the Word and the hope of Jesus. She felt the Holy Spirit. That spirit connected with her, and the harvest will come when it's time.

Before we were able to walk away, the women asked for their pictures to be taken. That request spoke volumes to me. It was as if they were saying, "Take my picture so I can be seen, but I'm not allowed to be seen." Seeing Papa bristle at the request, I quickly snapped a photo so not to upset their Papa, smiled, and walked away as they said, "Nakupenda." I love you.

All too easily Doyle and I could have been fighting that man with an axe and he would have been well within his religious rights to do so. We were trespassing on his land, with his family. He, in his beliefs, perceived us as a threat. He had friends and fellow villagers that would have come to his aide long before they came to ours. But by God's grace, we did not end up fighting for our own lives. Instead, we offered them a way to fight for their eternity. It was the peace of God's presence and the covering over us that did the work. We just showed up.

When spiritual influences are threatened such as was the case with Papa and the influences that he entertained, there is a tangible battle that reflects the spiritual battle within. From his perspective, the Christians were a threat to his beliefs, but what was greater was the agitation that was created as carriers of Jesus entered the enemy's atmosphere. However, when we know our authority and we execute it with love in the name of Jesus, a supernatural coverage exists.

Our interpreters have not experienced this kind of battle before. There was no yelling, defensiveness, or aggression on our part. Yet we were unmoved, secure, and firmly in control while being completely unarmed and outnumbered. That's not earthly, that is supernatural, and that is the hand of God in action.

When we left "Papa's" hut area, I turned to Doyle. We exchanged a look of solidarity, but we knew not to gloat or do or say anything that might be construed as disrespectful. We knew our mission.

Keep it Moving

We continued to walk from hut to hut, repeating the announcement of the Good News. Doyle and I were privileged to lead family after family in their choice to dedicate themselves to Jesus, even amidst the surrounding conflicts.

It's no exaggeration in the fact that there were so many people wanting to know more about Jesus that we lost count. The sheer number of people and families that chose to renounce Islam and accept Jesus was so large in our daily walks that our interpreters were not able to record all the names of those we talked to. We didn't just invite these wonderful people to accept Jesus and then leave them unguarded. Records were being kept by the interpreters to provide them with the support and teachings of Jesus that would lead them to a deeper relationship with God.

It was magnificent to see the book swelling with names and desires for hope to be nurtured in Christ. I'll never forget walking over to a home with at least a dozen children standing out front. Doyle was within sight but headed to another hut. As I approached the hut with the children, a woman came out and stood holding a cloth. As I stepped up to the doorway, the children surrounded me in every direction. To assure the children that there was no threat, I smiled and extended my hand. Immediately, I could see that all the children were sick.

Their noses were all running from both nostrils down to their lips. They coughed such deep chesty coughs that the Mother in me just started to pray. Their struggle to breathe was nothing foreign to them, as they seemed to be mostly unfazed.

"Habari" I said with a smile. I explained to her, through my translator, who we were and that we were there to tell her about Jesus. She dropped her head and seemed exhausted by the simple statement. She exhaled as if she had been holding her breath for days, as she shifted her weight and leaned on a post.

"I'm a Muslim," she explained. "There is a sick man inside that is Muslim," she continued. She was extremely conflicted but not saying anything more. She glanced at the door that she just came out of.

"I'm here for you and these children to know of Jesus Christ."

She seemed very concerned for my safety, glancing back into the hut at the doorway. She never made a move to walk away but she kept a constant eye on that doorway. Lowering her voice as much as possible, she explained the struggle she was facing. "The Muslim man inside is likely to come out and chase us down if I were to accept Jesus," she explained.

"What do you want for you? To be Muslim or to be Christian?" I probed.

Her reply actually caused me to blink twice. She explained, "Inside, I hope to be Christian, but outside I am Muslim."

We heard a rustling inside the hut. She and I both shifted our eyes to the doorway. Her nerves were suddenly at the surface, "Please come back when it's safe. I want the prayer of Jesus, but it's not safe now."

I could see the exhaustion in her eyes. I could see her turmoil looking at me and then looking into the hut. I looked at the number of children that stood between her and I. By quick glance, seven or eight of the children were at vulnerable ages from two to ten years of age. She knew this man and she knew what he was capable of. Even in his sickened state, she was full of fear. I could have pressed forward but she and the children would have been in harm's way, not to mention how he might respond to a white, female, Christian American.

I acknowledged her trepidation and nodded.

I told her that she was loved either way and walked away to preserve her safety and the safety of all those children. As we left, we waved at her and all the children. I noticed that none of them made a choice to go back into the hut. They didn't walk away to play. They just stood there, glued in place, returning waves with smiles that went from ear to ear.

The danger here is very real.

We are doing what?!

Oh, let me tell you this, when we walked up to this next location, in the flesh it felt like it might be the last time anyone saw me or Doyle again. It was a fortress, and no one knew where we were. It was a yellow compound that was surrounded by metal gates and concrete walls. Both of which had metal spikes affixed to them as a barrier between the people inside and the very real threats from outside world. Oh, and did I forget to mention…*razor wire!*

As I looked at the size of this compound, I marveled at the money it must have taken to create such a place. This part of Africa is not known to have any affluence whatsoever. So, "What were we about to enter?" I wondered to myself.

This would have been the first time the slightest portion of apprehension began to creep into my spirit.

There was no knocking mechanism. No way to announce ourselves, except to pound and yell into the compound. That is precisely what my translator began to do. I stepped back and gave wide berth to whatever was on the other side of this massive gate.

After a few moments of yelling, a sweet, small young girl opened the gate just the smallest crack, then quickly turned away and ran as fast as she could back toward the concrete building inside. We pushed the gate open slowly, not sure what was on the other side that we could not see. Even then, I knew it was crazy that we were entering a sealed compound, in a foreign country. But why not, I mused to myself.

With that, we stepped forward into the sealed area as I took inventory.

- No one knows where we are because we had wound our way through unmarked villages over the course of hours.
- The gates are way too tall for us to get out.
- We don't speak the language.
- And I only have one good arm...

Yep, this seemed like a great idea. Let's go in. All I could do was laugh as I did the mental check list in my thoughts.

Back in the United States, this would have seemed like a suicide mission. No one of sound mind would have walked into a closed, sealed, compound with barbed wire, spikes, and concrete walls, but...this was a different world. In many ways it was so easy, free, peace filled, and anointed with God's presence all the while defensive mechanisms reminded us that here nothing is as it might seem. Turning away was not an option. Not because it would have been rude, but because we were there on a mission that only God could have determined. We would see it through. In other words, it would have been crazy NOT to go in.

The gates must have been weighted because once we stepped inside the gates, there was a heavy metallic thud signifying that the gates were now officially closed. So there we were, standing at the entrance of this compound. Alone. No one to greet us, and the child that darted away was nowhere in sight. In fact, there was no movement sensed anywhere. We stood quietly and just listened for movement or sound within the compound to give us a clue as to what to expect.

After several very long minutes, a man began to approach us. His face was stern for a young man in his twenties. Immediately, our interpreters began speaking out our intentions in Swahili, "We are here in the name of Jesus."

Others began to file out of the house. They heard our announcement. Hearing such, the young man who was leading the approach nodded. However, his face did not change. He was clearly choosing to not give any indication about how they felt about the Christians being in the compound.

After some quiet consideration, the oldest sibling motioned us toward the center of the compound and just said one simple word, "Yes." He waved us to follow him as he we walked to the back of the compound. We were not taken into the house, but to an area behind the house that was covered by a tin roof. Once we were there, they turned and walked away without any word. I looked around at what we could not see from the perimeter. We were surrounded by walls that rose six to seven feet in height and topped with razor wire. No one is getting out of here unless the owners wanted them out.

As they began to make their way back toward us, Doyle and I turned our attention back to the people who escorted us in. They had chairs in hand as they motioned us to sit. More people began to flow out of the center of the compound, and I heard the sound of the metal gate in the distance. No one was talking, everything was silent, yet peaceful movement. It was very strange by American standards.

Suddenly, we were joined by the local residents. An older male, four children, and an adult female which they referred to as their neighbor. It was then the silence came to an end, and we learned of where we were at.

Half of them knew about "this Jesus" and the neighbor was a Seventh Day Adventist.

Armed with this information, we began a dialogue that was open and honest about the promise of God. We watched as one of the young girls, who appeared to be in her early twenties, began to display sadness. Extreme visible sadness. When she arrived, her appearance already indicated such a depressive state, but as we spoke, her sadness increased.

I asked the Lord what was going on here and it became clear. She was being convicted in her spirit. Not by what we were saying but by what she was feeling. Doyle was speaking in those moment that I took notice of her grief. I sat quietly watching her become more and more uncomfortable. It became almost unbearable to watch as she began to squirm, and her face contorted with pain. I put my hand on Doyle's leg to stop him from speaking. (A signal that he and I developed in the United States that kept me from having to interrupt his thoughts.)

Immediately, Doyle recognized the signal and stopped speaking, and turned his face toward me. Seeing that I was focused on the young lady, he turned back toward the young girl. "What are you feeling?" The question was simple but complex in every way. She was having trouble expressing what she was experiencing, so I repeated the question. "Tell me, what are you feeling inside of you right now?"

Her reply was a determined statement from her lips but something inside of her was fighting. We could watch the manifestation of the fight within display itself on her face one twisting grimace at a time. "I need prayer." Her voice was strong and precise. She continued in Swahili, "I need THE prayer of Jesus." Emphasizing the word "THE" as clearly as possible with the language barriers in place. "I've had enough of the life I'm living. I need the prayer of Jesus." She expressed to us that she knew that only Jesus could give her the peace that she sought after.

We asked her if she knew what that meant to believe in and accept Jesus in her heart and her life. This was a question she didn't take lightly as she considered her options and her thoughts. She restated her decision, "Yes, I want this Jesus."

We were all too happy to assist her in her request and the change was immediate. I don't know what she was running from but by the time she said, "Amen," she had the most beautiful smile and the most loving light shine through her. She literally began to bounce around and dance in her chair at her choice.

All the faces suddenly changed from stern to reflecting the atmosphere that just made itself known. Others were now asking for more prayer of coverage, protection, and blessings of Jesus. They were going from knowing OF Jesus and being aware of speaking Christian prayers during their conversion over the years, to embracing the fullness of hope that was being explained to them that day. All were smiling and all were now shaking hands in their customary repetitive way of acceptance. Voices now lifted with laughter and gestures of open arms with statements welcoming us back at any time. It was almost head spinning to consider we walked into a cold, unwelcoming compound, where we stood alone and were escorted with grim faces, to this jovial social setting in which even the children were dancing around us with joy. Only God could have done such a thing. We just kept experiencing one miraculous moment after another. However, the biggest was yet to come.

We stood up, signaling our intention to depart. As we did, they returned the body language to escort us back out of the compound. Doyle stepped back assuring that I got out of the gates first. Once outside the gates, I kept moving forward but I had only made it a few feet when I passed a young man in a light blue shirt. In my spirit I received the word, "him."

Obediently, I looked back to advise Doyle about the man in blue, but as I turned around, he was not behind me. He had been stopped by the same young man in the compound that we had been talking to. The young man was struggling with sexual issues and needed a prayer that he could not request in front of the women and children. It wasn't out of shame that he was concealing his request. It was out of honor. He was following a code of honor. A young man who recognized he was wavering in his sexual walk, stepped away from the women and children to pursue his own healing. Not because he was pressured to, not because he felt obligated to, but because he wanted something for him to get closer to God and he didn't want to speak "inappropriately" in front of women and children. There is something so loving and respectful in that choice. Such an intimate choice to please God and a desire to respond to God's loving direction and correction. He requested that Doyle give him a moment in private to pray for staying strong and free of sexual sin.

Since Doyle was tied up, I doubled back and began speaking to the young man in the light blue shirt. I showed him the flyer that indicated we were talking about the festival in the area. He advised, "I'm Muslim. I'm not going to the festival." Hmmmm, I know the Lord prompted me to approach this man, so what was up with his aggression? "I know who this Jesus is. I'm still Muslim."

I accepted the initial pushback and just showed him that I loved him with a smile that truly came from my heart. That action bought me some time to ask the Lord quietly how to proceed. "I respect that you are Muslim. Can I share with you some stories about Jesus?"

After careful consideration with his arms crossed and a bit of fire in his eyes, to my surprise, I heard him say one word. "Yes!"

My brain was immediately searching for which stories to tell of Jesus when my mouth just began moving independently of thought. Before I knew it, the man was visibly weeping, and I was telling him of Jesus' assignments for him in his life. He responded with yes after yes. God was moving my lips and choosing the delivery on messages that I was just there for. After I stopped talking, he was still visibly affected.

"How do you know these things about me and my life?" he said with an awkward smile, almost sheepish.

"Through the Holy Spirit."

We began a dialogue of what the Holy Spirit was and how we can live with this divine connection daily if we love Jesus and desire Him to be the center of our lives. He stood there just staring at me. He didn't move. He was frozen in contemplation, frozen with the inability to know how to ask for something that was igniting inside of him. He put his hands on his chest with tears in his eyes. His mouth opened but no sound came out as he hung his head.

"Would you like me to pray for you?" I asked.

Without a single word he held out his hands.

"Would you like to accept Jesus in your life as your Lord and savior?"

Again, he was frozen. The conflict was waging inside of him. It was written on his face, and his body was almost paralyzed. This was a classic flesh versus spirit battle. It's very real.

I pressed on, "Would you like me to pray the prayer of Jesus?" His hands remained out but silence and tears brimmed his eyes. "Would you like to become a Christian and leave behind your teachings of Muhammad?"

This time he answered, "Yes, I want Jesus."

I'll never forget the look on his face and the loving connection in his eyes. He never looked away from me. He held my gaze. He was so determined to accept Jesus he was trying to speak the English words rather than those of my interpreter. He was desperate. I stopped him and said through my interpreter, "Relax, you can't get this wrong. Speak in your language and mean it from your heart. Not from your head."

I watched as he took a visual deep cleansing breath and his grip on my hands relaxed. Again, he focused on my eyes and mine on his as he repeated after me in Swahili what he now knew to be true in his heart. Afterwards, he wiped his tears and said, "Jesus is now my Lord."

It was about that time when Doyle joined me giving a word to the young man. His smile was radiant as he walked away, turning to continue to wave.

As we walked, I took a moment to praise God's loyal connection to us, even when we are tired, hungry, or distracted. God knew that young man in blue was one of his children. I didn't, but God did. I just needed to listen. God will stop at nothing to alert his children to his presence and desire to be accepted and loved by them. He will stop at nothing to show his loving care and protection over his children, including having some American woman double back and talk without fear to a man who is openly displaying aggression toward her.

But God knew the words. God knew the key. God knew his heart and God knew his conflict. --- Game over Satan. God wins.

Find "The One"

We had been walking for hours. I was getting tired, and it was hot. We had entered another village. And yes, it too was Muslim. We wandered up on several families sitting together on the ground, some on blankets and some were just in the dirt under a single tree. It was quaint and calm regardless of the fact that there was at least twenty of them in such a tight space. The irony was with this quaintness and calm was also silence, no levity, and no joy. There was heaviness in this setting.

There were several older women watching us approach. There was a wiliness in their eyes. They were sizing us up, but their hands never stopped moving and the movements were incredibly subtle. It was obvious they had seen some conflict in their lives, and they knew they were surefooted in it.

The younger women were excitable and welcoming, and the children looked between the older and the younger to discern their own response. Such an incredible balance of youth and wisdom. Most remained seated as we walked to stand just a few feet from their blanket. "Habari," was the word that came from my mouth but the thoughts in my head were, "Lord help." You see, the older and wiser woman began to send warning glances to the younger women and their body language began to fall into order.

Ignoring the wall that they were putting up, I began to address all of them collectively. Doyle and I found it worked best for us that I initially address the women and he initially address the men. I felt Doyle behind me and was going to introduce him, but before I could, my spirit kept being pulled to one woman in the back. In this kind of setting, its best to never single out one person over another because it can make them a target in their Muslim community, but the spirit was strong and could not be ignored. "I'm here with the festival. We are teaching about the life of Jesus."

It was as if they were trying to actively block out our presence. They began talking amongst themselves and going about busy work. I was undeterred. That same woman had my attention as she worked on preparing whatever food item she had in her hand that she was cutting apart.

I spoke again, "We would like to invite you to the festival."

It was then that one of the elder women spoke, "We are Muslim." She never missed a beat in her handiwork. The woman clearly had the respect of everyone here. What she said goes.

It was now as if we were shunned. The women began to talk as if we were not there and they wandered off as nonchalantly as possible, while children ran off in every direction.

I thought to myself, "Ok Lord, tell me what you want me to do. Move on?"

Instead, this strange sensation moved over me. What dropped in my spirit was equally as intriguing and probably a little bit stupid by earthly terms. There was a heaviness in the spirit of each person not wanting to be the first person. Yet I saw a curiosity that was coupled with fear. But what the Lord had dropped into my spirit was a boldness that was almost impossible to express. "Who Lord?" was my simple question. As they continued to keep busy and block out the evidence of our existence, my spiritual eyes went back to the woman in the very back that God illuminated. It was the same woman that got my attention when I walked up. At no time did she ever raise her head, yet I knew she was THE one that I was there for.

I pointed to her and said, "I would like to talk to you." The voice that came from me was like that of a stranger. I was surprised at the authority that came from my mouth. Her head raised suddenly at the tone in my voice. I had no intention of singling her out and less than zero intention of using that tone with her or anyone else.

Something was about to occur in the spirit, and I was just along for the ride. Noting my tone and the authority that they just heard, those that had wandered off now reconverted at the blanket. I felt my posture change absently as I stood up straighter, but I purposely softened my tone just a bit as I said to her, "May I come sit with you?" Never rising, she agreed to allow me to sit with her by a small almost frightened bobbing of her head. She never stopped working with her hands, but the entire scene changed. As I walked closer, one of the elders dragged a stool out from an adjacent hut. As I sat, she raised her eyes and her head to look at me.

Her hands stopped moving for the first time since our arrival, giving me her full attention. The moment she did so, there was a tangible electricity that entered the atmosphere that somehow worked well with the peace that was spreading through my body. I recognized that feeling. Something in the spirit was about to be annihilated. A woman in a white head scarf that had swirling circles (as seen in the photos) sat next to her.

When Kingdoms Collide

As I began talking to her, it was as if nothing else around us existed. It was her and I. I was so focused on her that I didn't notice that all those who had scattered or busied themselves before, were now gathering around us and they had brought even more people. They were in front of me, behind me, and to either side of me. I was surrounded and never noticed. That electric that flowed was God's supernatural powers and it was surging while creating a calm.

Without warning, the woman dropped her hands into her lap only to raise her gaze to look at me with such pain in her eyes. Although the pain was there, she continued to listen intently. When I finished talking about the grace of God, I looked at her and sat quietly. She sighed and took a deep breath. No one moved. No one said a word. It was as if the world had stopped.

Unbeknownst to me, the crowd had grown considerably and surrounded me. Somehow, every single person was as silent and did not move a muscle. The long pause was intense, but no one was willing to break what was happening. God was doing a work and we were just there to witness it.

After what seemed like an eternity, she opened her mouth and began releasing her pain. Through the interpreter she spoke, "My husband died in February (just a few months before) leaving me with five children and a Mother to care for." She motioned with her hand to the hut and toward the children. It was only then that I realized we were surrounded by children and young adults. "It is his Mother, and she cannot walk because she is old, and he left us," she explained.

"I am angry with your Jesus!" she expressed quite forcefully. "I am angry with your Jesus for leaving me in these conditions without food and without a father for these children." She was now free to speak, and she could feel it.

"I am angry that your Jesus left us without protection of a man," she said as she openly wept. "I have no husband. I have no future. So how can your Jesus be a good Lord? Your Jesus abandoned us; your Jesus left us with this. We are burdened and alone with much to carry."

She took a deep breath before she continued. "I have shed many tears because of Jesus. How could He be a good Lord?" She determined that because she was in pain, God had turned His back on her during her time of need. She went on the express that her anger was justified, "Jesus has failed to protect me."

The crowd began to increase as I sat on this little stool and watched this woman release pain that could not be contained. I heard movement as an older woman behind me sat in a doorway of a hut listening and watching with intensity. Another woman stood just outside of the gathering, leaning in to hear as much as she could. A quick count yielded a minimum of eleven children had gathered. Almost falling over those who had lined up in front of her, a woman in a black head wrap and black dress clasped her hands behind her back but leaned underneath the tree toward me to hear as much as possible about this Jesus.

"Tell me your name," I requested. She quickly obliged. "Jesus does not want you to be alone. Jesus never left you." I gestured to the crowd as I conveyed, "These women and children around you are not to be burdens but instead they are gifts in your life because you are not alone." As I spoke, her spirit was absorbing what was being conveyed and my interpreter had much trouble trying to keep up with the flow of the Sprit that was breathing life. "My sister, please understand, Jesus grieved, the Lord God grieves too. Do you know about the crucifixion and resurrection of Christ?" I asked.

"Yes."

"Do you know that the God of the universe and the stars cried when Jesus was on that cross? Do you know that Jesus cried out in pain? Do you know that His pain was created so that we could be protected from the enemy and evil?" As I asked these questions, she sometimes nodded and sometimes cried. "My sister, He is a good God because he grieved for you before you ever existed. He knew you would hurt but He is also the same God that sent you these messages. He's calling you back to him. He loves you, and Jesus is the pathway back to him."

She began to cry again. She was shaking her head trying to process all that I said. It was then that I acknowledged the crowd. I pointed to the many children unsure which of those were hers and asked, "Do you consider your children a blessing?"

She said, "Yes."

"Would you do anything for your children?"

She said, "Yes."

"Do you know that your children will have some heartaches and pains to live through as they grow up and mature?"

She said, "Yes."

"Do you believe that there is much that they will learn and grow from during those hurts and pains?"

She took a moment before she replied, "Yes."

"Would you ever leave your children?"

She said, "No."

"Then my sister, what makes you think that your Father in heaven would feel less love or would do any less for you?"

Silence filled the space between me and her. It was almost as if a lightbulb just went off in her eyes. Suddenly, she understood. Another long pause took place. Her eyes cleared of confusion. We sat in silence as God continued to work within her. My interpreter slid me a glance as he waited for instruction. She raised her eyes up to the tree above her only for a moment before she looked me directly in my eyes, "I think I'm ready to forgive Jesus."

In that short sentence she spoke, there came a scurry of activity. I raised my gaze to survey the surroundings. To my delight, the children moved in closer until they were almost falling over one another. In the photo of me sitting in that chair with my interpreter's hand suspended in the air, that is the moment that the children began to mouth the words of Jesus. They were riveted at this God. God was planting seeds again. This time it was in these children.

With the fundamental decision to forgive Jesus, we began to pray together and ask Jesus for guidance in her heart, her hands, and her mind. The children mouthed the words with us. We asked for love for Jesus to be reignited and for Him to make himself known to hearts in a very new way. While she was accepting Jesus with a fresh and new understanding of who He is and will continue to be, the children were saying the name of Jesus with intrigue and curiosity. I was looking at future Christians.

God had found the "one." The one that was ready. The one that was designated for this day. The one that was ready for this appointment. God saw her pain and sent someone. THAT is a good, good God. Never alone, never abandoned, and never outside of His sight. Our Father, who art in Heaven and very much with us today. The Children would follow but only as allowed to do so in their Muslim homes...that is UNTIL they cry out to Him quietly and silently on their own.

Before I left, I told her I loved her. Her response was so genuine, she smiled as she spoke, "Nakupenda," while she rubbed on my hands with her hands to convey the love she felt.

As we said goodbye, I looked back and saw the smiles of all those who heard the word.

We Were Being Followed

Throughout the day, I had this feeling of being watched. I would turn and look every now and then but saw nothing. We are always being watched from a spiritual realm perspective, but this felt as if we were being physically tracked, followed. There was nothing we could do about it, so we just kept walking as I alerted Doyle to what I was feeling. He turned and looked but also saw nothing.

I turned to my interpreter, "We are being followed."

"An animal?" He inquired.

"No, it feels human," I replied.

We continued to walk, speaking to people as we made our way through the villages and countryside to our pickup destination. We weren't alarmed because ever since the news of my partner and I had spread throughout the villages, people began to show up, follow us, and listen from a distance.

It was getting late in the day, and we needed to get to our rendezvous point. If we were not there, the pickup car leaves. We had already ran into that little snafu once and really didn't want to deal with that again.

There was a footpath between two mud huts that we ventured between to expedite our exit, my focus being on the car that I hoped was waiting for us. Because of that focus, I stopped looking behind us for a while. When I realized I had gotten distracted, I turned again. This time I saw who was tracking us. Walking between two more huts were two sets of eyes.

I recognized the scarf that was wrapped around the head of one of those sets of eyes. It was the young lady with the yellow head wrap, and she brought someone with her. They had been following us from place to place, ducking into and around huts and corners, watching intently from a distance. Not sure what it was these young ladies were looking for, but they were enamored by something that they could not express. I turned and waved so that they could know that I knew they were there.

You see, in that setting, you never truly know who is a friend and who is just a really good actor for the enemy. Staying aware is critical but living in fear is not an option. There is no formula for interacting with people in such an intimate way. Just as Jesus did, every encounter was generated by something that God placed into motion. You can't plan these interactions. You can't use logic. What we have to work with is what God provides, flowing in the spirit, and letting Him close the gaps.

We stayed out on the streets daily from 8:00a.m. until 2:00 p.m. The interpreters assigned to us kept record of all those who chose to convert to Christianity and accept Jesus as their Lord and Savior. This list served as a way for the churches to find the people again and offer them the support that they desired in learning more about "this Jesus." The list was getting so long none of us anticipated such a response. Page after page was filled. It was nothing less than supernatural. Doyle and I had become the local celebrities in the streets which increased our abilities to reach the people. Now they were coming to find us, but the longer we were out, the bigger targets we became.

Matthew 4:19-20

"Come, follow me," Jesus said, "and I will send you out to fish for people." At once they left their nets and followed him.

Our Lord and savior, the King of Kings and the Master of the Universe is a tremendous God. In as such, He was moving the hearts of the people to find us when we couldn't get to them. We were only going to be there for ten days, and ten days doesn't allow for all the ground to be covered that we wanted to cover take place, but God had that worked out as well.

The people were now coming out into the streets in droves to find Doyle and I in order to learn how to get close to Jesus. Think about that! That is such as crazy thought. We were being pursued so that they could find a way to pursue Jesus.

Late one day, Doyle, me, and our interpreters walked down a dirt footpath. We were getting tired. The heat had become a bit rough out on the dirt pathways as it stuck to our skin from perspiration. There was no breeze and we ministered for many hours with no breaks for water.

We were getting close to the end of our day when we heard a woman's voice yelling from a distance behind us. The yelling continued, so we turned around only to see a young lady in her late twenties running after us waving her arms to get our attention. We stopped, not knowing what was so needed and so urgent. She was in distress.

"What do you need sister?"

She was winded from the run, so we waited for her to catch her breath. "I want Jesus and I want Him now." It was that easy and that concise. "I want Jesus and I want Him now." She said that she had felt us going down her street and she felt inside of her that she needed to find us.

"It is something inside of me here (as she pointed to her chest) that told me I needed to hurry and find you."

She was right. Our time here in this village was coming to an end and our day was getting ready to conclude. She did not know this, but the Holy Spirit did. She was being called and she responded without delay.

"Why do you want this Jesus," was Doyle's question. It was important that she understood what she was asking for.

"I need Him," she said through tears. She could express what she felt by the way she held her hands over her heart. Doyle and I understood. With a nod of Doyle and I, all four of us moved toward her and surrounded her. In the following few moments, we taught her a bit more about Jesus before she recited the prayer accepting Him into her heart.

She was very emotional as she learned more and more about Jesus. She responded with such anticipation and hope in her eyes.

"If you are ready to accept Jesus as your Lord and Savior, hold out your hands," Doyle said to her.

Without any hesitation, she did exactly that. She repeated word for word with tears rolling down her face the "prayer of Jesus" as they began to call it. With the final word "Amen," peace flooded her. Her smile filled her face. She smiled and gave out hugs of gratitude and heartfelt love. And just like that, she returned to work with the rice and grain.

Luke 13:24

"Make every effort to enter through the narrow door, because many, I tell you, will try to enter and will not be able to.

The Manipulation Begins – Jezebel

After another full day, we returned to our team and met for a late lunch at a local restaurant. We shared about our experiences and the love we openly expressed and received on the street.

However sweet the rest of the team was, I noticed a spiritual shift in one of the women. That same woman was now openly staring at me. She was now suddenly very clingy to the lead evangelist of our team. Purposely hanging on to his every word and smiling really big when he was around, but as soon as he was distracted, her smile crashed in record time. This didn't feel sexual. This felt manipulative.

"This is going to be a problem," I thought to myself, but I was not to say anything…YET.

As we all sat and swapped the stories of our day and experiences that we each had with the people in the various places we were at, unexpectedly, Rachael, a team member that was sitting with us who we would come to know as Jezebel, said to me, "I want to go out with you guys one day."

My spirit was almost uncontainable in launching the word…"NO!" out of my mouth. I managed to keep the response quiet, but I also knew if she went out on the streets, I was not going. Yet I had NO idea why, only that's what my gut was telling me. It felt like a warning…and it was.

Several things were VERY clear on this trip.
1. The spiritual atmosphere was surging and influencing people at unimaginable rates.
2. It wasn't just the Holy Spirit; it was also the dark spirits. There were collisions occurring between dark and light at every twist and turn, but the biggest were yet to come.

That evening, Doyle and I were talking, "I'm craving some foods we are used to."

"Yeah, I could use something a bit Americanized right now," Doyle said.

With a smirk on my face and a mischievous look in my eyes, I spoke, "You know I have beef jerky, tuna, and some goodies in my suitcase."

He smiled, "I have a few things too. Meet me in my room and let's go nuts."

We laughed and without a word we were headed back to our bungalows to grab the familiar noshes that reminded us of home. It was like two kids in a candy shop. We threw everything on his bed and began to survey our options.

Settling on tuna in pouches, we began to create a meal from whatever we had. Dumping little packets of mayo and relish into the foil packet, we began to pass it back and forth. Just the taste of it on my tongue was heavenly. We both flopped back on the bed with contentment and couldn't help smiling. Probably glowing.

That tuna didn't last too long before we busted open the next food item, and then the next, until we were so full, we knew we could finally get some sleep.

As I stepped outside of Doyle's bungalow to head back to my own, Rachael was standing outside.

Why was she standing there staring at his bungalow? Hers was next door but her hands were together on her cane. She had been standing there for a while, "I heard you laughing. It sounded like you two were having a good ole time in there."

She was standing there listening and watching. "How predatory and creepy," I thought to myself.

She snarled as she looked me up and down and turned without another word and walked away.

I was not going to let her get to me. Her issues are not with me. Her issues are with her own issues. I turned and walked the other way without any word to her. My stomach was full, and I was tired. That was all that I was concerned about.

Anyone who doesn't know your character or treat you according to your character, will judge you based on their own character. Her accusations told me more about her than she intended.

Church Unchained

Sunday

Sundays were amazing days. We were each sent to local churches to preach a message that was near and dear to our hearts. Each time our measures of faith would be tested, as we didn't know what church, what location, who the pastor was, who our drivers were, or if our interpreters would meet us at the church.

What we did know is we would all be separated in order to cover as many churches as possible. We knew we were to meet at a central location and a driver would show up and take us to the location of where we were to preach. That's it. We knew nothing more.

It probably was a bit more uncomfortable for me since I have a history of being kidnapped and beaten. But overall, I think it's safe to say it's a strange sensation to have no idea where you are going, how you are going to get there, who you will be with, how you are going to get back, where you will be taken to afterward, or what time it is to begin or end. Just knowing that you are to go, speak what Holy Spirit says, and go with the flow of whatever follows, sounds bizarre but there was a freedom and peace I had when there was absolutely no visible reason for it.

The priority Holy Spirit was laying on my heart was to preach the Gospel and the desire of God to have a relationship with each and every person.

It was then that a driver showed up. Of course, he did not speak English, and instead pointed toward the car I was to climb into. The problem with that was…there were A LOT of cars in that general area.

"Well, I guess this was the car that he pointed to," I thought to myself as I climbed into a stranger's car. I closed the door behind me and waited.

I hope they received the instructions of where to take me and that they were not just filling their own agendas. "That would make me hard to find," I giggled at that thought. It was so weird that even at not having any information, I had no reservations.

Arriving at a church type setting, I was driven to a back door. The driver got out and motioned for me to get out as well. It was then that a man came out that same door and began to shake my hand in their customary format. He was their Pastor. He motioned for me to follow him. The sounds that came from this church could be heard quite a distance.

The praising words for "Yesu" (Jesus) just permeated every dust particle and wooden beam.

When I walked through the door, it was as if I had stepped back in time. I was in awe.

The children danced with all their might at the praising of God. They sang praises to God at the top of their lungs. Men danced wildly, openly, arms and legs flying high in praise, reaching toward God and completely unchecked by their appearance. Women danced wildly with babies strapped to their backs or in some cases, danced while the babies were latched onto their breast to feed while they praised.

Their love for the Lord just brought tears to my eyes. Such innocence untouched by our cultural restrictions of what is acceptable. This was not religion; this was a hardy desire for relationship.

There were no personal platforms of fame, or social media here. There were cries of the heart that come straight from their soul. It was beautiful.

As I preached the message of relationship between God and us through the connection of the Holy Spirit, I was shocked to learn that none had heard of anything like that.

As I glanced out over the congregation while preaching, I looked over at the Pastor for signs or signals of when to wrap up my sermon. But what I saw was the Pastor taking notes as quickly as possible, nodding and writing. On occasion, he openly grunted (the cultural sound of approval) and following it with the approving nod.

It was on my heart to share about His character and His heart to connect with His children. He wanted so desperately for them to know He's not a tyrant waiting to be served. I was overwhelmed at the emotion that welled up in me after seeing their eyes riveted into the thought of an inner connection of the supernatural love. A love that was in place before they were even on this earth.

I saw for the first time the depth of their distress. They were all too familiar with and accepted that superiority comes with a demand of fear. They knew the witch doctors required fear and reverence and they had transferred that same understanding to Jesus.

They were taught that God was a supernatural being that ruled over them. And just like the witch doctors, one that had to be appeased. They didn't know the love and intimacy of the creator of the universe.

I was shocked.

The message was so well received that the people were brought to tears, including the Pastor himself. When I was finished at the pulpit, I walked over and sat down in the chairs designated for the guest. The Pastor of the church took his place at the pulpit and just stared out over the congregation only to turn his full attention to me. Looking at me, he spoke the thoughts that he had been considering, "We, I, this church, has not been taught that we can have a relationship with God. We only read about Him," the Pastor humbly admitted in front of the entire church community. "This is a miraculous statement!" he continued. The Pastor was visibly overwhelmed.

"Please Pastor ma'am would you come back up here and pray for us?"

He motioned for me to return to the pulpit and alter. I agreed. However, as I approached, my heart broke at the desperation of these people's desire to grab onto what I had preached.

Without a word or an invitation from the Pastor a woman came up and quite literally sat at my feet, looking down, never glancing up. She was so close to my feet that I could feel her breath on my legs as she coughed.

I asked my translator, "What does she need?"

My interpreter responded, "I don't know. I will find out."

She would not look up. Even as the interpreter asked her to raise her head so he could hear her. Her head hung down staring at my feet and touching them while sitting on her own knees. I felt her desperation.

When my interpreter came back up to my side, he announced over the singing and praise the cause of her distress. "She has active Tuberculosis. She is in a lot of pain."

I nodded my head in acceptance of what he had said. Apparently, that is all the motivation that the congregation needed to come up. Half of the church was now lining up at the platform spanning from wall to wall at the front of the church. One by one, people began forming a row behind that row, and then again behind the second row began a third row. They just kept coming. Every single person stood patiently holding out their hands ready to receive whatever the Lord was ready to deliver.

The next few moments were a blur of spiritual decisions that didn't require any thought. Only movement and connection. (I had to review a video that someone from the African church took of me to recall all of the following events.)

I looked at the woman who came and sat at my feet. She had since begun to stand up to prevent from being stepped on by the congregation pressing forward. I began running through my experiences and my religious teachings of what the proper way to handle such a crowd should be. What prayer might be best for these people who are so in need? Before I knew it, I had just entered into thinking in the flesh and allowed religion to get in the way of faith.

I raised my hand to the woman's forehead. She was coughing and expelling every bit of her energy as she coughed. As the coughing subsided, she brought her gaze up to mine. Tears lingered in her very unhealthy looking eyes, until she closed them. With tears of pain streaming down her checks, I reached up and I placed two fingers on her forehead.

My translator began translating my English prayer. Now the battle was tangible. There was something in the atmosphere that was holding it's ground. The woman was unmoved and looked at me for an explanation but said nothing. My translator just looked at me with anticipation as the crowd began to grow. More and more were coming in the door, adding to the already packed church. The pressure was on...Until I got real.

You see, I have been casting off dark spirits and laying hands since I was a child. Yet when I became an adult, the churches began to dictate what they felt was acceptable and "proper." I had let that get into my head.

I closed my eyes and went deep into the teachings of my Holy Father in heaven. My Yeshua. I learned to lay hands back when I was still holding a teddy bear and the Lord prompted me to put my hands on it and pray. I grew up Methodist, so laying of hands and spiritual languages were something I had never seen, known of, or experienced as a child. I received the spontaneous baptism of the Holy Spirit alone as a teenager and it scared me to death, as I had no idea what it was. When I was in my 40's, I began attending churches that spoke of these things. However, all but one of those churches tried to restrict me with religious rules and regulation. In other words, earthly compliance.

But now, standing in front of all these people and understanding the battle in front of me. It was time to go back to my roots.

I abandoned all restrictions of religious proper conduct and flowed freely. Again, I raised my hand to her forehead and began in English, and before I knew it without conscious thought, my prayer ignited into a new tongue. One that I had not heard or prayed out before. The moment it came out of my mouth she went over like a falling tree. This was demonic and had become a rescue mission. Instinctively, I reached to catch her, completely forgetting that my shoulder was only able to hold ten pounds without dislocating and didn't have any range of motion, let alone the ability to reach out and forward while bearing weight. The shoulder not only worked, but it also held 100% of the woman's weight as I laid her down…Miraculous!

I stood back up and looked over at my interpreter. We surveyed the number of people who were standing there waiting for my prayer over them. My interpreter was overwhelmed as he asked, "What do you want to do?"

I laid down the microphone that they insisted I hold and replied, "Divide and conquer."

All religious teachings, rules and regs were scattered as I instructed him to go one way and I walked to the other side of the church. He looked at me from his side of the church while standing in front of the people waiting for my cue.

I gave him a nod and I raised my hand to the next woman's forehead. He did the same and began praying in Swahili, whatever the Lord laid into his spirit. However, since I had no interpreter, I went directly into tongues.

If I had not seen the video myself, I wouldn't have believed the responses that took place. A middle-aged woman that stood next to the woman I had my hand on fell over with a scream while the woman who's head my hand was on remained standing. At this point, the demons were revealed, and they were sorting themselves.

Possession versus oppression…yep, the demons were not hiding, and it was getting sorted out. Just wait, it will become clear….

Moving from person to person, men and women began falling at a rate that was almost incomprehensible. Sometimes the spirit was so thick just a wave of my hand in front of an individual while reaching for someone behind them caused a response.

I walked over to another woman. I raised my hand while in my prayer language and without notice or contact, she fell immediately without any concern for her own safety. Again, my shoulder was able to lay the 150-pound person down to safety.

The villagers didn't know English. Not even one of them. So, prayers in English were just noise without meaning. They couldn't respond to something they didn't understand. But when the prayer tongue ignited, the people didn't need to know what I was saying because...the demons recognized it. It was a prayer that only God issues and a language that the enemy feared.

Remember the woman who didn't respond to the hand I laid on her? Well, I went back to her with my interpreter after things calmed down. I asked her, "What did you need prayer for?"

"I want to have a baby, but I cannot," she replied.

It was then that it made sense...those who responded were said to have been dealing with the devil, fighting major ailments, or something similar. Those who did not respond just needed prayer for food, clean water, a baby, or guidance.

God sorted it all out. No translator was needed. God's presence sorted everything.

I didn't have much time to assess the miracle that took place in my shoulder, tongues, or the people because as I turned around to sit, people began handing me their babies and their children for prayer.

These were not gentle requests. The scene had changed.

"Mama Pastor, you are a real woman from God that gives prayers that scare demons. Take my child. Save him."

They were not asking. The desperate mothers were crying out for help. Children were being thrust at me from arms that appeared out of a crowd of people. It was impossible to see who the mothers were. It was just a sea of need. As children were popping forward from the endless reaching arms, I was able to reach out, grab them, raise them up over the heads of the crowd, and place them in front of me for prayer. I would then yell out "Mama!" and the woman would come take her child as another child would appear from the arms of the crowd. This repeated many times before a small baby emerged from the arms of the crowd. The baby was very small, weak, and didn't make a sound.

The crowd parted and allowed for this one woman to walk up to me. She placed the baby into my arms and my eyes filled with tears. "Pastor, my baby…is she dying?" The words were heavy with pain and fear of the answer. My heart was breaking, and my mothering instincts took over. The baby, once in my arms, urinated all over the skirt I was wearing and was unable to hold up her head.

I asked, "When was this child last seen at the clinic?"

"They sent me away because I have no money," she declared.

This was a story I heard all too often while there. Either the issue was transportation, money, or they just didn't understand what the clinicians were saying to them.

Again, I looked at the child and she appeared to be small. Small enough for me to wonder if she was a preemie when she was born. However, as was the case with everyone we asked, no one truly knows when they were born. This was no exception. The mother didn't know how long ago the baby was born.

"Your baby needs to go back to the clinic for more food and more water."

She looked at me with loss in her eyes. She had many more children, no one to care for them, and her food was limited. She replied, "The journey is long, and I have many children. They will again send me away. Please pray."

"Mama, if I pray for your baby, will you promise to follow my instructions?"

After a long pause, she nodded and verbalized the word I needed to hear, "Yes."

The baby was not crying. I cradled the child and rubbed the bottom of her feet. She responded and opened her eyes. She was breathing very well, her eyes were clear, but tired. I wrapped the child in the loose dry folds of my skirt as I prayed over her. The translator repeated the prayer to the mother so she would understand what I was praying. The mother stood listening to the prayer and crying with all that she had inside her. Her other children pushed forward to see their sister and what the mother was crying about.

Once the word "amen" was spoken, I turned and spoke directly to her, "Mama, listen to my words."

The Mother nodded quickly with hope.

"Your baby needs to be fed more times a day."

The mother expressed that she fed her when she cried but she hadn't cried much.

"Mama, your baby is very little and cannot wait for crying."

The mother pointed to her own breasts and expressed her feelings of failure and probably depression. With her hand on her chest, she said, "They do not give what the baby needs sometimes."

Understanding what she was saying, I explained, "Then you must try more times a day. This baby needs more food, more…everything."

"Will God not heal her?" She asked.

"Yes, God does and will heal, but you must do what she is needing you to do. Just as you eat, she must eat. Just as you drink, she must drink. God heals but you must provide her what God provides to you. Ok?"

"Yes mum," she conveyed.

It was in that moment that the baby started to cry and wiggle in my arms. Her mother was so elated in that moment that she scooped the baby off my lap and began yelling hallelujah, disappearing into the crowd. I never saw her again. When I was back in America, I was told that the woman had returned to church with the baby several weeks later and the baby looked strong and healthy, but that was all the information I could get.

After service, the Pastor led me outside the front door of the church. Suddenly, he asked me to stop and stand off to the side. The translator told me to stand and face the church doors to be greeted.

"What? Greeted? I just preached for more than an hour." The thoughts were just barely finished in my head when suddenly, one by one, sixty or more people began to file past me. Each one breaking out in a united group song.

Each person adding to the song as they exited the church.

I asked my interpreter, "What is going on? What is the song about?"

"It's about honor and thanks."

Oh wow, they were honoring me. I watched as each person curtsied, bowed, hung onto my hand, or kissed me on each cheek to show their acceptance of me while the singing continued.

There was so much activity I almost didn't notice the boy on the stick. I had not seen him during the church services, but this time, he had my full attention. He brought one leg forward and then swung the stick in front of him. Bracing and balancing his weight on the top of the stick, he maneuvered through the footpaths, uneven ground, and gaping holes of the terrain. This was not a crutch. It was truly a limb that was broken and jagged, but he used it as his leg. The boy only had one, the other was missing. He hobbled over to me singing as the others did. He reached across his little pre-teen body to find my hand and give me the customary African handshake of respect.

This was his normal. This was his life.

After each person passed by, they stood next to the person that came out before them and created a huge circle of singing and dancing. Each person to follow walked down the line and showed love to each person they touched in the same manor. After everyone was out of the church, we all congregated in a circle outside for parting and encouraging words that they would carry forward through their week.

I watched as they walked away singing.

"Wow, how beautiful," I thought to myself.

Again, without explanation, the Pastor motioned for me to follow him. "Where are we going?" I asked my translator.

However, he motioned to me that he could not explain yet with a subtle nod of the head.

In response, I nodded my head and began to follow the Pastor away from the church and away from what was familiar to me for the last hour. I was making mental notes in case I needed to walk back to the church. "Ok, we are walking past the church, onto a dirt footpath that is only as wide as my shoe, past the chickens and livestock…" These were my thoughts as I continued walking into the unknown and the wild.

We walked and walked and walked. So much that keeping track was no longer a possibility, so I gave up. There were various types of structures and common areas with chickens walking over my feet and between my ankles as we walked. Several common areas consisted of many people sitting outside their huts on the ground thatching or preparing their food for lunch or just milling around preparing for the next moments of their day. There were buckets of unknown plants and vegetation and a woman preparing a fire. Waving hello to each person I passed, I figured, "Well, if I don't know where we are going and my translator is behind me and I can't ask any questions, I might as well make some friends."

The Pastor came to an abrupt stop and pointed to a doorway in the side of a mud hut. "You go in there," was the instruction I received, but I still had no idea why. I did so without hesitation. My interpreter was right behind me but turning to ask him "why" was not an option.

Walking through the doorway, I was careful to watch my footing. The floor was earth, so it was very uneven. There was

When Kingdoms Collide

evidence of washout either from the rainy season or when they dump used water.

I saw a place to sit across the room and through a makeshift doorway. Walking over to it, I was giggling openly at the baby chickens, which freely roamed and walked into the house with me. Momma chicken was watching closely as it became clear to me. "Oh!" I realized at that point, "this is the Pastor's house." I had looked back for my interpreter but lost him somehow between receiving my instructions to enter the doorway and walking into the hut.

Having no ability to communicate, I took a seat and placed my hands in my lap, waiting quietly, and alone. Believe it or not, being in an unknown place, without the ability to communicate was very peaceful. My cell phone had no signal, so I was on my own in the truest sense of the word.

But there was such beauty in this. The weight was not on me to entertain or uphold any dialogue. I was merely there for whatever God was doing. That's it.

Finally, my interpreter came through the doorway. He explained that the Pastor would like to honor me by having lunch prepared for me.

"Thank you but for security reasons I am expected to be back at the place I am staying at 2:00 p.m."

My translator quickly dismissed that statement with a wave of his hand and continued, "We must not dishonor him by leaving before he serves you his best meal. This is our culture, and we must accept his hand of honor."

"Okay doke," I mused to myself. I was at their mercy in this circumstance. I shrugged my shoulders and said to my interpreter, "I guess I might as well enjoy the ride."

"Ride? What ride?" my interpreter asked. He is a native to the area so not at all familiar with some of the phrases we use, so I quickly dismissed it, "It's an American way of saying this is fun."

He accepted that and nodded, turning to sit in a chair facing me to my left.

So, it was clear. Was I going to be back in for check in at 2:00? Nope…I was going to be late and couldn't do a thing about it except smile.

I heard the sounds of food being prepared. I looked at my phone. It was 1:30 and I had learned that meals take hours to prepare here. I entertained myself by watching the rooster join his chicks and their mama, while I quietly sat on the sofa speaking to my interpreter.

The Pastor wandered in and sat for a moment. I asked my interpreter to inquire, "How do you feel about today's church service? What did you think?"

Through my interpreter he spoke, "People do not get to hear that kind of teaching in Songea. God is using you in a very different way that will change the way people think and feel about God."

I was so caught off guard, "Thank you Pastor."

With that he stood, "I must go check on your meal."

As I was trying to process what he said about the teachings in this area, all of a sudden movement caught my eye and Danielle was entering the doorway. "Yes!" I thought to myself.

Danielle was part of our team, but she had been sent over to another location to preach. Each of us were dispersed to cover more ground. Danielle sat down with me, and we talked a bit while our food was being dished out to us.

Danielle is a wonderful woman of God; one would think that she could not be fooled by the enemy...right?

Pay attention my friends...ALL, even the elect, can be fooled. Take note the movement in the enemy in the coming chapters.

We watched with curiosity as our plates were filled with what appeared to be rice, bananas, greens, and their version of what we thought was beef. (However, later we were advised that it was most likely wild rat. I guess we will never know.)

Our hosts and their family mounded our bowls with each of these food items and watched eagerly while we ate all that we could. To this day, I find myself smiling as I recall the looks that Danielle and I exchanged throughout the meal. We were very grateful for the hospitality, but we were unaccustomed to what we were trying to eat.

The meat was not something either of us could tear, chew, or swallow whole. It was brown, beyond tough, and basically impenetrable. We were not about to insult the hospitality, but we had a dilemma.

These wonderful people, who have no running water, no electricity, poultry and animals running around their houses freely, sat and made a meal that was most likely their finest food. They sat waiting for me to finish to make sure we were "satisfied." They didn't take one handful until we were almost finished.

Their love for hospitality and each other's wellbeing far outweighed anything I had personally experienced here in America or anywhere else I've ever traveled.

Danielle looked at me as we tried to navigate the food options gracefully.

At some point, they had all left the hut except for me and Danielle. "I can't chew this. I'm not sure what to do with it," I said.

"I'm not fixing to choke in Africa, so try to tear it," was her reply.

Neither of us could, so we ended up digging a hole in our rice and depositing the meat items inside the holes. Probably not the classiest move but we didn't know any other option.

Ultimately, we made it back to the place we were staying and settled in for the afternoon.

Friendly Fire

Up to this point, there had been small collisions with the dark forces of evil, but the enemy was getting more agitated at our presence by the minute.

You see, Doyle and I were a pair of vessels that were breaking down barriers and doors between the Muslim community and the Christian community that we were not supposed to be able to break. We were breaking the barriers, opening doors, and creating bridges where there was once only animosity and territorial behaviors. Needless to say, this did not please the enemy but I'm assuming that it pleased my Holy Father.

Dinner was full of laughter and joy. We each exchanged the stories of the message we delivered and our experiences with the beautiful people of the churches we were at. We began swapping stories and showing photos and videos of our day. It was light and happy. It was full of God and His love. That was until…Rachael sat down and began to manifest Jezebel.

I was starting to feel the Lord begin to alert me to the depth of this woman's manipulation and hatred for me, but I made a conscious decision that I would not let her drag me into her anger.

Rachael sat next to me. She is a woman I love dearly, but I knew in the spirit did not feel the same about me. I was ok with that because that was between her and God, not her and I. What I don't believe she understood was that since it was between her and God, once she manifested Jezebel, God would stand tall in shutting it down and correcting the spirit within her. It wasn't my job.

She sat with her arms crossed at the table and didn't say much for a while.

Generally, she was very kind to my face and always seemed to urge me forward in my ministry and gifts. In the past, Rachael had requested many times for me to lay hands on, in prayer and support, and love on people who were guests at her meetings.

So, when she asked me how my day at the church went, I was only too happy to share my joy. As the video played, I saw her face fall and change. She watched as the video captured people being delivered and others just being slain in the spirit with peace played out before her. I would have thought that she would have been so happy for those people, but Jezebel, as usual, cannot contain herself. Jealousy stepped in and reared its nasty head.

She now had a callous grim face with a forced false smile. I saw that she was going to turn on me. So, in an effort to keep unity, I asked, "How was your preaching at your church today?"

She leaned forward with her elbows on the table. Her response still rings in my ears as she sourly responded with the same callous snarl, "Not like yours."

She went from being chatty to silent. Those were the last words she said to me the rest of the meal. She was suddenly ice cold, openly drawing her elbow away from my direction, putting it firmly into her lap as she looked me up and down. I remember thinking, "What was her problem? She's been in healing rooms and deliverance rooms. Heck, she's even run them and participated in them."

Jezebel was at full manifestation, and I was her target. The dark-haired woman from my dream had just revealed herself.

The switch had just been flipped and so it was to begin. The spiritual battle had just launched and now I just had to wait for her move.

Jezebel can't sit still for long. She seethes and connives until she can't contain herself. I had no idea what method of attack she would use, but I was one hundred percent sure she was coming for me. But I knew something she didn't…God had already warned me and now God was about to handle His business.

Strength Under Siege

Going out to walk the villages for hours every day, and in some cases all day, was beginning to wear my partner and I out. We had no place to get out of the sun, we had no place to rehydrate ourselves, and there was no particular stopping point as we just kept moving until we couldn't walk any further.

This particular day was exhausting. I turned to Doyle, "I'm wearing out. Between the combination of the schedule we've been keeping, the sun, and all the walking, I'm bone tired."

Doyle expressed the same, but as any good partner does, he encouraged me to just close my eyes at dinner and he would wake me up to eat. He must have seen how tired I was because during dinner, I literally could not keep my eyes open. I tried to prop my head up on my hands just to keep it up. It was obvious to everyone.

"You look so tired," said one of the men that sat across from me.

"I am." Such a simple reply but I felt the words so deeply.

Jezebel heard the conversation as she watched us dialogue back and forth. She was watching closely, as if she was sizing me up. She was on the prowl.

I slumped against Doyle as I repeatedly closed my eyes and said to him, "I need sleep. I can't go any further."

Surprisingly, it wasn't Doyle that responded, it was Jezebel. She spoke in her most convincing tone of concern, "You don't look so good. You need sleep."

At this point, I should have noticed that I wasn't hearing the woman I had grown to love, I was hearing the voice of Jezebel through sneering words. I was just too tired to notice and part of me felt that I was surrounded by Pastors and Ministers so surely they would see it …right?

As we sat for many hours waiting for food, we used that time for both debriefing and delving into many other conversations. Since there were so many of us, in my tired mind, all the conversations melded together and became a blur of sound.

Once I finished eating, I was not able to function any longer. My only focus was wondering when the next transport car might arrive. The thought of returning to the bungalow, showering the dust off from the day, and closing my eyes in a bed was a small slice of heaven.

I had not remembered being this fatigued in a long time. As soon as the car came, my partner and I climbed in. I wondered why the car had sat waiting, but I didn't have to wonder long. Jezebel made her way into the front. Doyle and I looked at each other. We knew something was up. Doyle grabbed my leg subtly to let me know he was sensing something, and I gave a gentle nod to convey I had the same feeling, but we knew to keep quiet.

The ride was completely silent until we finally got back to the place we were staying. Doyle and I got out of the vehicle and slowly walked toward the courtyard between the bungalows. Turning to Doyle, I said, "We should probably grab a bottle of water from the bar for tomorrow morning."

He agreed and began to approach the bar which was just a few feet from me. He slid me a glance as we both noticed Jezebel walking slowly and with purpose toward us when her bungalow was toward the outside of the campus.

She had an agenda and Doyle and I both felt it. I felt the prowl on her, but I was just too tired to care. I had just told my partner

I was heading to my bungalow and started to walk away, when low and behold, Jezebel began to put her agenda into action.

This took planning. This took thought. She was not just having a whimsical moment of wanting to chat. She was about to compound her lies. Jezebel was now moving swiftly in the spirit. Jezebel was about to make her move, but she didn't know I was ready.

The Battle Before the War

"If You Only Knew"

Jezebel strolled up to us and donned a smile on her face. "Come to my room tonight for a girl's night" she insisted.

"I'm tired," I said and declined her invitation, but she wasn't going to take no for an answer.

"All the ladies are coming to my room tonight. We are going to hang out and have some girl time," she continued.

"All the women?" I purposely asked.

"Yes, they are all joining me in my room for some long overdue girl talk to just relax for the evening."

Doyle looked at me, and I was sliding glances to him. We both felt the deception. It was like talking to a snake. I tried desperately not to go up in tongues at her presence.

Jezebel was determined to attack, and she picked the night that she saw just how tired I was. Typical Jezebel behavior. Jezebel is an opportunist, and she found her opportunity.

"Ok, let me drop off my things and I'll walk over."

With that she seemed satisfied.

Doyle looked at me as he walked me to my bungalow, "You sure you want to do this? You know she's up to something."

I sighed a huge, exhausted sigh and replied, "I might as well deal with whatever predatory attack is looming. She and I will go face to face."

"You think that's wise as tired as you are? I'll go with you."

Doyle looked at me with concern and compassion as I said to him, "There's a reason why she segregated you out. She's going to attack me. She specifically chose the words 'girl's night'. She's actively separating us; she's coming after me."

Doyle's jaw moved in anger and frustration, but we were thousands of miles away from home, half our team was still at the restaurant, and it was late into the evening with a sky full of stars watching from above.

I could have so easily rejected the invitation, which on the surface would have been the easy way out, but God was working something. I just had to trust the Lord enough to take the ride.

Once I dropped my things off in my bungalow, Doyle and I continued walking over to Jezebel's room. He walked me up the steps to her bungalow, waiting while I knocked. Sensing the spirit in front of us, he again asked, "You sure you don't want me to stay?"

"No, this is my battle. She's gunning for me, not you." I just wasn't privy to what direction she was going to take the battle into.

The door swung open and Jezebel more than sweetly said hello to me. It was like saliva dripping from the lips of a jackal, as she was satisfied that her prey had arrived at her door. It was as if she didn't see Doyle initially because the moment she did, she didn't even try to conceal her disgust. She dropped her tone several octaves and let the icy words slither off her lips, "Oh, hello." Her tone was cold and angry. She turned and walked back into the room, leaving the door open for my entry.

Doyle grabbed my hand and squeezed while looking me directly in the eye, "You sure?"

I knew he was giving me one chance for him to come with me, but Jezebel's mask was now off, and the battle was now on.

I nodded and said, "I'm sure."

"You going to be ok?" he asked.

I nodded that I would be, all the while Jezebel stood inside the room. "She'll be fine, it's just a girl's night," came the voice from inside.

I confirmed I was fine and with that he turned and walked away.

It was almost time. The strike was coming. I just had to be patient.

I stepped into the room and met her tone with one that let her know I was aware. "You said this is a girl's night. Where are the other two ladies on the team?"

She visibly bristled at that question and said, "They are coming, don't worry."

"All of them?" I pressed.

"Yes, they are all coming. It's a girl's night."

It was just her and I as Jezebel closed the door.

"So where are they?" I inquired.

"They will be coming along later, but this will give us some time to catch up."

"Nope" I thought to myself. I'm not saying a word to this woman.

She sat staring at me without saying a word for a few moments, looking me directly in the eye as I sipped my bottled water in silence. I guess she decided it was time to break the silence. "We have quite a bit to talk about," she said with a smug look on her face.

I stopped drinking my water long enough to reply to her saucy sentence. "If you only knew. But I thought you said we were going to relax tonight," I said with a look on my face that matched the challenge on her own face.

"You know, people who are impure shouldn't be on this team," she said dripping with accusation.

"I wholeheartedly agree," I lobbed back at her.

"You know, those kinds of people should be silenced," she said looking me directly in the eye. Jezebel just threatened me. At that point, no matter how tired I was, I straightened my posture both in the flesh and in the spirit. I was not dealing with a woman that I could love, respect, or receive. I was dealing only with a spirit that will be rebuked.

"I think this conversation is over until the other women get here," was my reply.

"Why? You got something to hide?" the accusations continued.

I decided to just confront her, "If this is about your jealousy issues regarding my friendship with Doyle just…say it."

She literally snorted sardonically, and I knew. She was jealous and she was going to try to take me down to feed her own issues. She either was attracted to Doyle and scorned that he showed no interest, or she was jealous that she didn't have a Doyle in her own life and somehow that made me her target.

Suddenly, there was a knock at the door. Danielle had arrived and I was hoping I was wrong about the evening plans. Danielle was my friend. I could trust her to look out for me…right? She wouldn't partner with this evil…right?

Upon the entry of Danielle, Jezebel resumed her performance of fake pleasantries and banter.

We were still missing a woman who was on the team and the missing woman was the leadership over the women's conference. Jezebel's ministry position was subordinate to the missing woman's position. If this was legit in any way at all, why would she not be in attendance?

When Jezebel shifted into her performance of pleasantries for the other woman, I was frustrated to see Danielle's response to her was niceties. I realized they were on the same team. It was then I settled in knowing she was moving forward with her plan. I was about to be ambushed by two people. I was tired, but I thought to myself "game on."

Right before Jezebel began her rant of control, I felt her shift from this woman who I've known for several years, a seemingly loving, soft, and compassionate person to something distant, cold, and agenda based. I could see in her eyes and hear in her tone that for some unknown reason, she believed, albeit falsely, she was in some sort of power seat and was going to use it to push her own personal agenda.

I was stunned to hear the next words out of her mouth.

"You're too loving toward people," she said.

"Excuse me?" I retorted. I noticed she was generalizing at first but that wouldn't last long.

She then referenced Doyle and began accusing me of being too loving toward him.

"What are you talking about? He and I have been ministering together for years. Long before I ever met you"

"And on top of that you're too bubbly. You need to tone that down."

Her statement was almost laughable. This woman is known to have one speed, slow. One attitude, cocky and one mood, sour. "You want me to be more like you?"

Her answer was simple, "Yes, I've learned my lessons already."

Assassinating my character and trying to remodel my personality into fitting hers apparently wasn't enough. She wasn't done yet. She was just warming up. "All that smiling, laughing, and hugging. And you shouldn't say to people Nakupenda" (I love you) to 'these people here.' It's just not proper."

Needless to say, my thoughts were, "Who do you think you are?" I was disgusted at what she was saying. I can't stand religious spirits and religious babble any more than Jesus could, and I don't have patience for demons who decide to confront me. You see, Rachael had suddenly morphed right back into Jezebel. A vile, twisted, walking, talking lie. She proudly went on to inform me that she was acting on the "direct and specific authority of leadership," which was also later to be found as a bold-faced lie.

Jezebel was trying to eliminate me for some reason. This was personal! For some reason she decided she did not like me, and she was going to make every effort to hurt and wreck me and my ministry, even if it meant she was going to use deceit in the name of Jesus.

"You know, there's thing about being too kind. It's a result of being engaged with impure spirits that are looking for personal satisfaction."

"WHAT!?" This had just gone from crazy to insane. There was something deeply wicked about this woman's mind.

The spirit of perversion had just entered the room. Apparently, Jezebel had defined compassion, connection, and loving our brothers and sister as too kind. Holding someone's hand when they cry, giving or accepting a hug, looking into someone's eyes when they speak through their own pain are now suddenly "too kind."

Disgusting. She was actively trying to violate Jesus' direct rule of human conduct. According to Jesus Himself, we cannot separate our love for mankind, our neighbors, and our brother and sisters from the Love we have for the Lord. Because if we do not love our brothers and sisters the way Jesus loved His children, we cannot love the Father. And if we love the Father, we also love our brothers and sisters.

Jezebel was specifically telling me not to treat people the way Jesus would have treated them. Now there are some that will try to minimize what Jezebel "meant" by her statements, even make excuses for her wording or timing, but let me be the first to tell you, this was planned.

Remember my dream of life being sucked out of me? The dream that didn't occur until we arrived here. It was a warning dream to prepare me for this assault that was right here, right now. The Lord knew that Jezebel was going to try to intercept to make my mission a failure. However, the Lord warned me to armor up and that He would stop her. God's plan would not be stopped.

Rachael's ministry (as Jezebel or not) may be cold, unfeeling, and distant, but mine will never be. The war was now clear. This was a war against the one thing that Jesus bled for, the one thing that Satan doesn't have a weapon against, love. It's a battle to stop love. I could feel the eyes of the Lord lower into the direction of Jezebel, much like a librarian looks over her glasses to scowl. Jezebel didn't know the fight she was actually fighting wasn't against me. It was against God.

Jezebel was always against loving people and this Jezebel spirit is the same. The spirit of Jezebel never changes, only the participants and circumstances change.

It all made sense now. Before the trip, the Lord had showed me images of me kneeling with people on the ground and ministering to those in the most need. He warned me not to shirk back. Now I know why. Because the evil that was with us was on her own mission. To stop me.

As the nonstop babble came out of her mouth, I couldn't help but smile at the inaccuracies and the contradictions in every statement. The nasty spirit had her tongue and she no longer made sense. There was no reasoning with her or this spirit. This had to play out. Part of me wanted to feel sorry for her and blame it on the spirit, but that's not the way it works. If someone wants to keep their demons, they get to do that. That's a conscious choice to partnership with evil. For that choice there is no pity.

As tired as I was, I stuck to my position and reminded her that we are supposed to show each other love by our actions. That Love by God's definition is a verb. His love is full of action in our daily lives. "We are ordered to love one another and love our neighbors in the scriptures," I said.

She snickered at that statement.

I continued, "God is Love. Jesus loved openly and freely. Joy is one of the fruits of the spirit."

She continued to sit there with her arms crossed in defiance.

Love is such a big deal to Jesus that the word "love" is mentioned over three hundred times in the Bible but has no value to Jezebel. She was deaf. Her mind was perverse. She had made her choice. The Kingdom of God and Satan's kingdom of earth were colliding…again.

The Battle Rages On

Unconscious Sin Revealed

Her own perverse ways of thinking corrupted her ability to process anything clearly. Jezebel's shell was starting to crack under the weight of her own manifestation and lack of control, when she made this statement, "I've walked down that road before in one point of my life. It didn't end well."

Boom! There it was. The reveal of her own guilt and wounds that she was trying to pass onto me.

I couldn't help but wonder, "What did she do in the name of love or affection to or with another that caused her so much anger, even hatred, and desire for destruction of another human being?" What I do know is the impure heart that she was accusing me of, was actually a projection of her own. She, by her own words, "walked down that road" of impurity in the church and now she was targeting her jealousy, anger, and bitterness on me, attempting to derail God's mission.

This was a direct and purposeful choice to partner with dark spirits and she was indeed partnering. So deep that this woman, who prays for people and knows the Word, couldn't even recognize the way she was in direct violation of God's word.

Control was immense in the room as Jezebel didn't take but a single breath between sentences and threw around crazy accusations and circular arguments. Each sentence contradicted the previous statements she made. Never asking any questions, just a full-on rant that was ugly and revealing. Everything inside me wanted to launch into shutting down this vicious spirit of darkness, but I was reminded by the Lord that He was going to deal with it, and I needed to stay out of His way.

Jezebel continued, "I'm strong and I want to be part of a strong team."

She then pointed to me and said, "You shouldn't be here."

"Ah ha!" I thought to myself. We are right back where we started right before Danielle arrived.

Incredibly, Jezebel continued down this twisted, deranged path of attack for a long time. When I realized that she was not going to let up after 45 minutes of her spewing her nasty venom, I set my jaw and let her choose to cross the line with me. All the while, I endured her demonic, oppressive, and harm wielding attack. I closed my eyes and sighed as I was leaning totally on Holy Spirit to keep me in a Kingdom place while my flesh was being torn apart.

Anyone who knows me, knows I'm a fighter. I've never shirked back from a battle in the spirit nor in the flesh. But in this case, the Lord warned me in advance there were to be spiritual consequences for her choice that would not be issued by me. It was not my responsibility to respond in the flesh or in the spirit. I recognized that this woman was no longer the woman I knew. Or perhaps this was the real woman and the other one was the disguise. But now she had given herself over to the spirits and was operating accordingly. This was her choice. The more she spoke, the more she revealed of her own spiritual lacking and hardening of her heart and the spiraling down of her own life.

Jezebel held up her index finger and thumb in a pinching movement, "You can't even stray from what is acceptable even this much," she continued during her rant. It was so sad to see a women of that age fail to know what she was choosing.

To watch this woman strike out at me as a result of her own personal imprisonment by this nasty religious spirit made me feel a sense of pity for her, but it was by her own doing and her own choice. At some point, she admitted that she was struggling with Pride but that it was already dealt with and something that she would continue to deal with. She didn't see that the spiritual door was still open.

The entire time Jezebel was speaking I could hear and feel the spirits within her. Each jockeying for position to rear their heads. Control, Jealousy, Anger, Pride, Religion, Envy, Attention Seeking, among other spirits, were all pushing past each other to get an opportunity to display their many talents at their perceived target.

What they were not ready for was my solid footing with Jesus.

"Enough!"

Jezebel was running out of character assassination material to throw at me, so she resorted to attacking most of the fruits of the spirit. Wow! This was so blatantly against God.

In her opinion, Love, Joy, Peace, Patience, Kindness, Goodness, and Faithfulness were now in question! She was openly displaying disgust for each of these all the while claiming that the leadership of this team was backing her.

She gave me her look of superiority and said, "I'm only doing this because I was asked to. The entire team feels this way." I will never forget the next question she asked me. "What makes you think you should even be here?"

Ignoring that foolish, arrogant question, I fired back and asked the questions the Lord laid in my spirit, "Who did *you speak* to about this?"

Her reply. "Just one person," and she named them.

"Who spoke *to you* about this?" I probed.

She named the lead evangelist on the team as the *man* who spoke to her about it. I could see she was lying her way through this so I continued as the Lord led.

I asked, "Who has a problem with the way I show love?" She said, "Everyone."

Hmmm, now how is that possible if she only spoke to one person and only one person spoke to her? More lies.

Remembering that this was supposed to be "girl's night" and that "all" the women were supposed to be there, I shot my reply back to her, "Why isn't Janice here to say these things to me? Janice is in charge of all the women and she's part of the team. You're not."

She said, "I was told to pull you aside and handle it myself."

"Interesting," I thought to myself because Janice wasn't the name of the "<u>one</u>" person she claimed she spoke to about this.

Calling her out on her lie, I said, "I thought you said that the lead evangelist is the one person that addressed this with you? And that's not Janice."

Jezebel stumbled over her words and drove the conversation in another direction to try and regain her footing.

Question after question failed to meet the mark of truthfulness. She was running out of steam; her story was starting to unravel. Her deep anger and resentfulness against the things of God had just about imploded.

Jezebel pressed forward saying, "If you keep gushing this love everywhere, what will people think?"

At that moment I was angry. I had taken all I was going to take. I looked at her with my fixed jaw and responded with, "Probably the same thing they thought when Jesus loved openly. When He, a single man, allowed a single woman to intimately wipe His feet with her hair in an act of love."

She just snorted in response. During this entire rant that seemed to go on forever, Danielle sat there quietly, barely moving at all.

I continued my statements, looking directly at Jezebel, "And just like in the Bible, those who didn't have the <u>spiritual depth</u> to understand the love in that action were indignant, yet Jesus defended her and defended the loving action. I will defend the action of love as well. Therefore, I will never deny another." I was incredulous.

At that point, Jezebel looked at Danielle and they began laying hands on me asking for my participation. I told them both no. And just like the dream, they continued regardless of my refusal. Regardless of my words of rejection, Danielle continued to lay hands on me, while Jezebel stood, watching, and making suggestions about how to "free" me.

Jezebel was using me as entertainment and Danielle was doing her bidding. As they laid hands on me, I silently began rebuking everything coming out of their mouths. I knew I was not to engage in this mess. So, as words were being spoken to me, I was praying against the spirit that was trying to suck the air out of my lungs and attempting to render me ineffective in my mission. So yes, I had to pray against whatever my friend Danielle was choosing to do to me. She was listening to Jezebel again and not to me. They would reap what they had sown, and He would allow and reveal the evils as He saw fit.

As I left the bungalow, Jezebel had one last request, "Let's keep this just between us."

Quite frankly, I was disgusted at both of them and didn't have anything to say to either of them, but I didn't miss the fact that Jezebel was scared of getting caught. "Why would she be so concerned if she was operating at a level of any authority for the group? Why would I be asked to keep quiet?" Hmmmm, confirmation that she was lying. "She knows she can be exposed now," I thought to myself.

I cocked my head trying to hold back my disgust and responded to her request, "Why?"

She replied, "Any disruption or discord to the team members could allow a door to be opened and a footing for the devil."

"If you're aware of that, then why did you do it to me?" Interesting, another contradiction. She's concerned for the others on the team but zero concern for the door she's attempted to open on me.

She was partnered with such evil she made no sense. I wanted to be forgiving and excuse away her actions, choices, and behaviors, but she had no repentance. A seventy-year-old woman in ministry showing no repentance or humility. This is dangerous. The spirit was in control. Jezebel had no idea how much of her hand she had been tipping, but I was too tired at this point and refused to deal with her clear confusion and manifestation as I shook my head at her and walked away. The audacity of this spirit aggravated me beyond words, but I had a responsibility to maintain my spiritual place.

To not tell Doyle why I was so upset after this evening would be a deception. To tell him and ask him not to say anything would be deceptive. She was actively trying to cover up her tracks. She wanted me to partner with evil and deception.

I refuse to partner with the darkness. Partnering with the deception would have drug me into an agreement with an evil spirit to participate in something that was clearly not of God. That in itself would have had long lasting results on the entire team. It would have opened a door for other spirits to access me. She was risking me, she was risking the team, and she was risking our entire reason for being there. Pure selfish evil.

So there I was, walking between bungalows at midnight. It was dark in the physical, but the spiritual darkness was trying to press in on me too. This was a predator. However, I would not allow myself to fall prey. I just had to endure.

Matthew 10:16

"I am sending you out like sheep among wolves. Therefore be as shrewd as snakes and as innocent as doves.

As I walked, I listened to the animals that sounded similar to wild dogs howling and yipping and growling in the not so distance. Mosquitoes quickly attached to me as I walked and knocked them off my arms and legs.

I looked up at the stars that were so deep into the sky and so brightly lit that they felt like I could reach up and touch them. I remember thinking, "Walking outside…at night, in the dark…in a foreign country…by myself, and no one knows I'm out here. Yep, this will probably go down in the books as the dumbest decision I've ever made."

I listened to all the other foreign sounds in the distance wondering what could make those noises. I made a mental note to bring a flashlight next time. I smiled and laughed at my thought. There will be no next time with that woman.

My next thought was, "God has this. It will be what His will determines and I'm grateful."

Once I made it to my bungalow, I was all too happy to get a shower and lay down for a night of warfare from all the spiritual vomit. She had unleashed such a spiritual attack on me that I fought the enemy in my room until 2:00 a.m. and notated every word I could recall in my journal. This would not end here.

Jezebel had done her best to open doors on me, to create havoc in me. She knew that the morning came with dozens of deliverances in witchcraft and voodoo territory, and she knew she was inflicting damage. At that thought, I fought the anger, resentment, the pain of her betrayal alone, in a foreign country, in the middle of the night, just like the warning dream I had before we left.

I fell asleep with tears rolling down my face as I spoke truth over the lies. "Father, my presence in Africa was preordained. I am anointed in this mission. The demons knew I was coming. Father, I believe that you will make this right."

Nothing any human, evil spirit, or any demon could do to deter me from my appointed mission. I held onto my prayer and my relationship with my Father.

The Plot Thickens

The next day, at breakfast, regardless of what Jezebel wanted, I told my partner of every single thing that occurred, and he was angry that I was personally targeted. Now our ministry was being affected. I was without sleep and as a result, unable to go on the streets to minister with him that day. Jezebel had won that round, but the battle was not over. I knew the Lord was doing something, I just needed him to hurry up.

You see, when we are tired and wounded, we want evil to be exposed. We want it now and often we step in front of God's plan and try to expedite our version of justice instead of waiting for His.

Everything inside of me wanted to reveal to the rest of the team that there was a snake among us, but I remained silent trusting that God was about to reveal a bigger picture and He would put the lies on display for the entire team to witness. I felt this strongly all the way down to my bones. I had to hold onto that hope and faith. This was between the Lord and her, and I was just the pawn.

But Doyle was different. We were partners. Anything that affected me, also affected him. I continued to explain the details of the evening events while they were fresh in my mind. No sooner were the words out of my mouth when he said, "I knew it! They are after you."

I shook my head and said, "Well, at least one of them is."

"No one has said one thing to me! Not one! This is a disgusting display of jealousy. I dare her or anyone else to come to me about what was said to you."

I was too tired to say much more, so Doyle picked up the conversation and asked the questions from there. "She actually accused us of having an affair?"

I shook my head, "That's just it, she was all over the place. She never said anything directly. It was like trying to follow the logic of a drunk."

"So you got berated for hours and she couldn't even be straight with you? So you don't even know what you are accused of?"

"Nope. She kept referring to walking down wrong roads and loving too much. I don't know, it was all just so insane."

Doyle saw the tears in my tired eyes and reached out to hug me in support and spoke into my ear, "This is bull$#*%!"

"Just keep it quiet until we see what God is doing," I said as people began to move about the grounds.

Even at the time of writing this updated version of the book, it's been over six years (Over two years after our Africa trip.) that Doyle and I have been together. We have ministered on three continents together in every kind of circumstance you can imagine. And to this very day, I have chosen to honor my vows to my husband and Doyle has remained a perfect gentleman. We are believers in the Lord's plan and that includes the purpose of our partnership and the direction of each day. Our loyalty to God and our mission outweighs anything and everything of the flesh. This level of loyalty, obedience and faith was something that Jezebel could not relate to, nor comprehend. That night told me more about her personal spiritual walk with God than anything she could have ever confessed.

However, that strained night in Africa, my fatigue and feeling the anger of what Jezebel was able to accomplish only sent me fuming, but I was not about to cause the rest of the team to be affected by the disgusting acts of Jezebel. She already affected me. I was going to protect the team.

While I was waiting for the team to arrive for breakfast, I was angry. I kept repenting for my anger but with every passing minute, it would bubble back to the surface and God and I were having a "What about me?" and "Can you hurry this thing up!" conversation. A conversation that is familiar to people all over the world.

When Jezebel joined the table, I was seething. She was right back into performance mode with an appearance of joy and being nauseatingly overly nice to Doyle right in front of me.

My seething rolled into total and utter disgust.

I took in the scene and thought to myself, "Talk about being impure. You're flirting with Doyle." I think I see her issue.

As people began to file in for breakfast, they began to notice my body language. I was not my normal joyful and free self. "You ok?" people would ask. However, either I chose not to answer or gave them a halfhearted smile. I wasn't going to act. That was Jezebel's forte. That thought was confirmed as Jezebel continued with a smile so large you could almost see every tooth in her mouth.

She spoke loudly to draw attention off what people were noticing about me and keep people focused on what she was saying instead. She knew I wasn't going to play ball by acting as if everything was acceptable. It most certainly was not.

The Lord told me to keep my mouth shut so not to create any disturbance in what He was doing or to the unity of the team. I received in my spirit, "Those who hear in the spirit will see her for what she is." So, I sat quietly and silently. I endured alone. Just me and my faith doing battle with the spirits that swirled around us. I knew that God was assuring me that those whose hearts were aligned with Him would see truth and leave the blind in darkness, wallowing in the spirits that they chose to entertain. I had to do my part. I had to stay low, humble, full of love, giving Satan nothing to place a foothold on. All the while, watching Jezebel take a perceived power position (Pride) with leadership, laughing and enjoying the banter of fellowship.

I was sickened as I listened to her as she was grabbing attention around the table with stories that I could feel were so empty and completely devoid of anything Godly. Surely these Pastors and Evangelists could see through this! Right?!...Right?! I prayed that they would see the truth quickly as I sat quietly, wrapped in my shawl.

I wrestled with contempt as Jezebel began to do the morning's devotional. I wanted to get up and put distance between Jezebel and I, but God told me to "stay put." In the flesh, I felt like I was being tormented but I refused to believe that lie. All the while, God stood right next to me. I knew what He wanted from me. Voluntary humility and surrender to His timing.

Unfortunately, Jezebel was not about to give up her "perceived" perch of power. That is exactly what it is, "perceived," because there is no power against God. It doesn't exist. She shamed the teachings of Jesus, she shamed the message of loved, she spoke falsely against an innocent party, she lied about her authority, and she contrived the meeting and manipulated to lure me in.

That wasn't one action, it was a web of evil.

There is no power that prevails against truth or love. There is no lie big enough or plot detailed enough to prevent God's commissioned soldiers from performing their duties as they have been instructed. God's Will will be done. He warned me the attacks were coming and assured me that He was handling it. That's all I needed to know. I'm on a "need to know" basis and I just need to stay out of His way.

I shook myself from my thoughts and realized the devotional topic was now opened up to an open forum dialogue for the rest of the people around the table. I lost track of the conversation and even lost track of where the targeted subject began and ended. I knew my time was coming at the table to speak and I had no idea how to respond. I watched as the third person to my right was conveying something and I tried to pay attention. I just couldn't focus on this, and I could understand why not. Was it fatigue? Was it anger? It was then that I very clearly received in my spirit, "Get ready."

I know my eyes went wide. God was teeing up to make a move and I had no idea what it might be. All I could think was "Uh oh!"

The man next to me now began to speak. He took his time before launching into a topic. It seemed like he was taking time to ask the Holy Spirit how to respond. You see, like me, this man receives in the spirit, so I know anticipation was all over my face as I looked at him. I knew the "uh oh!" came right before him so he was a key. "This should be interesting."

Suddenly, the man next to me, Mike, began to speak about something that I felt had nothing to do with the little snippets I heard of the devotional, so I KNEW something was up. My thought was, "Yes Lord, Yes!" He began to speak of how others judged him unfairly based on their inability to understand an individual's spiritual journey. And just like that I involuntarily launched with more power and energy than I was naturally producing. God was moving.

Vindication Begins

I said I agreed with Mike and "Sometimes, people in their own inability or choose to not understand another will instead judge and vomit all their own demons and baggage onto the person. Sometimes they try to force other people to carry their baggage of vomit just to lighten their own load."

I looked up and I saw Janice (the one who was missing from the "girl's night") looking squarely at me. I also knew Janice was spiritually strong and instantly understood. I was attacked and just like that, now **SHE** knew. Finally, the wheels were in motion. I locked eyes with her and watched as her jaw adjusted and her head bobbed up and down in recognition.

Indeed, God was moving…at least that was my hope and belief. At the conclusion of the devotional, nothing more occurred and it was time for the team to minister at their respective locations.

Jezebel positioned herself at the table and said quietly in my ear, "Don't worry. My report to Ashby is that there is nothing inappropriate to worry about." Oh, now she was realizing that her game was starting to fall apart, and that God was doing it. She was on damage control.

"Report? What report?" She was again invoking the lead evangelist as her go to.

I was seething. Inappropriate in what?! In loving the people the Lord led us to? In showing care for all that we spoke to? For holding the hands of those who wanted prayer? Of What?" She was going after my relationship with Doyle because of her own issues. I was now officially in the flesh and my only thoughts were, "Listen woman, Doyle and I have been ministering and traveling together for six years and have never crossed a line.

God had me approach this man that was unknown to me and tell him I would take a bullet for him, and you want to play God with God's assigned partnership?! The audacity!! Don't throw your trash on me."

My jaw was locked from clinching my teeth together in rebuke. My thoughts continued to reel from her pride, "Are you insane? Do you not see you are about to be exposed? And now because you realize that the team is on to you, you want to continue with this power play? Game on! Spoiler alert! My Father is Faithful! I will be redeemed!"

As I reflected on the cocky statement she made…"My report to Ashby is…," the righteous anger welling up inside my spirit started to get hard to hide. "Let me get this straight, last night she attempted to destroy me. Last night she flung accusations of loving openly and freely, of displaying the characteristics of Jesus and calling those characteristics inappropriate. But today is different somehow!? Interesting." The manipulation had just gone to a whole new level. Anger crept in, but I continued to keep my mouth shut while God did what God had to do to redeem me.

Mike was on to her. Janice was on to her. Doyle was on to her…This was a powder keg, and it was about to blow.

God had to have a plan. Until then, I would stay behind at the bungalow and rest. I returned to my room. I waited, I rested, I prayed, and was not at all shy with God about my displeasure at His timing. But, no matter how you look at this, this was an exercise in humility.

I struggled all day to stay connected to the soft heart that God gave me. The fleshly human side of me was wanting to lash out and go toe to toe with her, but I'm fighting to stay in my divinely assigned position of waiting.

That same evening, as I sat at the dinner table, Holy Spirit said to me one word, "Now!" and drew my attention to Janice's husband. I know my Lord's tone when He speaks to my spirit, so I bolted up out of my seat and followed him.

As I called out his name, he turned to me and stopped. It was then that I advised him of what was going on. He was clearly caught off guard. He was working in conjunction with the Lead evangelist and Mike. They were leading one leg of this journey. Janice was leading the women's conference portion (Rachel a/k/a Jezebel was actually under Janice's leadership.) and Doyle and I were our own leadership as we did the street ministry.

So, it was now clear, Janice knew there was a lie among the team and now her husband knew. The sweet man that he is began to comfort me with words of support, "I can assure you that none of what happened was authorized and she was out of order." With that, I took a deep breath and exhaled for the first time since the occurrence. He was now going to do what was right. He was about to take it up the chain of command.

Later that same night, as I sat in my pajamas, there was a knock at my door. Before I knew what was occurring, there was an impromptu meeting and my room filled with the team. All were in attendance except Jezebel, Danielle, and Ashby.

Over the next forty-five minutes, I learned of the extent of the lies in which Jezebel had participated in. I made it clear that I was not going to stop loving on people. I was not going to stop walking in unison with Doyle. I was not going to stop telling people they are loved, and I will not stop walking the way Jesus walked.

Doyle spoke up and said what I was thinking, "If this was about her and I, then why wasn't I consulted or spoken to?"

The room responded with various forms of, "You are correct."

Doyle continued, "This is a personal, planned, and targeted attack against her."

I looked at all those who were standing around my bed as they nodded their heads in agreement. After we said all that needed to be said, we adjourned the meeting and headed to bed in our respective bungalows.

Doyle stayed behind. "You ok?" he asked me.

I couldn't hold back all the emotion any longer. I sat and cried as he assured me, "You're a good woman. You haven't done anything to deserve this. This is not about you. This is about her and her demons."

As I sniffled and let the tears flow onto my bedding, I released the feelings of betrayal and breathed in redemption.

The next morning, before I met with my partner, I thought Danielle deserved to know what took place last night. I walked over to her bungalow and knocked on the door. She opened the door and in her sleepy state motioned me to come in. "Good morning, what's up?" she said after she cleared her thoughts.

I sat on her bed and began to unload in the nicest way possible. I told her of the meeting that we had in my room. I told her of the conversations that took place between Doyle and I. I put it all on the table. She sat there with her eyes wide. If she wasn't awake before, she was in those moments.

It was then that the Lord gave me the go-ahead to tell her about the dream regarding her trading her driver's license for a ring and sucking the life out of me. Danielle's eyes got real big and she put her hands on her face. It was then that she held out her hand. She told me that she indeed saw a ring at a **truck stop** when they stopped for gas one day and she had just purchased it. Confirmation! Confirmation not for me, but for her. She was actually wearing it at that time.

I could hear the hurt and the sincerity in her voice as she said, "I'm so sorry, but she said that she was acting under the direct instruction of Ashby."

I assured her of what I was told. "That was also a lie."

Again, she covered her face and said through a pained voice, "But she said it was by direct orders. I was tricked!" and "I was deceived by someone I love. I told her that I've never seen anything inappropriate between you and Doyle, ever." She shook her head.

I needed to know why she attacked me. "Then why did you believe it was ok to do to me what you both did?"

She replied, "I just believed she wouldn't lie to me."

"But you believed that I would have an inappropriate relationship?" I probed.

"I didn't know what to believe. She said it came from the top. But now you're telling me that was a lie too?"

"Yep…all lies. All of it," I snapped. I went on to say to her, "And you sucked the life right out of me that evening just like the dream said." Her face looked stunned as she began to recall the evening. She again looked at her ring…there was no way around this. She was lied to, I was lied to, there was confirmation for her, and I was warned before. This was evil in the works and Jezebel was recruiting. This is something that many people of God don't see coming.

1 Peter 5:8

⁸ Be alert and of sober mind. Your enemy the devil prowls around like a roaring lion looking for someone to devour.

As per our usual routine, my partner and I met around 7:00 a.m. for breakfast and prayer. Soon thereafter, Ashby joined us and asked if he could speak to me alone. He said he had heard about the ambush and explained that Jezebel was acting on her own accord and no one had any issues with me or how I minister. He apologized so deeply and so truly that I actually felt him loving me through this mess the only way he could. I felt his sincere support to my core. In truth, Ashby, the lead Evangelist, the one who extended the mission invitations to everyone, the one who everyone was expecting in Africa, was also blindsided by the accusations and actions of Jezebel. The pain that reflected my pain was in his eyes and I knew he meant every word he said. My heart was sorrowful for what he must have had to shoulder when he found out.

It was now over for me. The **entire** team was now behind me, but she had a lot to answer for.

To this day, I have not told Ashby or anyone else the rest of the accusations and lies that Jezebel attempted to attach to each and every team member. I knew it would not be conducive to anything positive.

I asked the Lord, "Do I tell them what she is saying about each of them?"

The response I received in my spirit was clear, "No."

Case closed, God's leading them, and they were listening.

The next day, a formal meeting was called. Each Pastor, four in total, advised Jezebel of their each being aware of the charade that took place at my expense. I learned that each of the Pastors questioned her and advised her of the injury that she had inflicted against a member of the team and how it affected the team as well as those I was assigned to minister to. To my surprise, as they restated those facts repeatedly to her, Jezebel was and remained unmoved. She was without compassion, without any response of repentance, sorrow, or empathy. It was apparent to all that she was an active participant in the darkness and was literally unapologetic about it. Everything now has been exposed and I have been fully vindicated. Glory to God!

Her hardened heart that allowed and continues to allow her to accept evil into her heart is between her and God. Remember...it's not people we are to war against, it's the principalities and powers that are influencing the people that we war against.

Ephesians 6:12

[12] For our struggle is not against flesh and blood, but against the rulers, against the authorities, against the powers of this dark world and against the spiritual forces of evil in the heavenly realms.

Demons Doubling Down

So here we go, now that the Lord vindicated me, Doyle and I jumped into the morning mystery vehicle and resumed teaching the Gospel to the people of Songea. We were prayed up, powered up, and ready to flow.

The devil ran into a roadblock. He failed to stop our mission using Jezebel because I stayed in my position and let God move. He tried using diversion, but we kept our focus. He tried using scare tactics, but we know no fear. He tried to separate Doyle and I, but we are loyal and steadfast in our unity. He tried using manifestations but that's just another day in the life of Doyle and I. Just like in the book of Job, the devil didn't know how Doyle and I would respond, but the Lord did. The Lord knows our hearts and our thoughts, the enemy does not. So, whatever my heavenly Father allows to take place in my life is fine, because I will not be shaken. And He knows that.

God knows all these things. None of these are tests that He anxiously needed to see the results to. These are for me and for the enemy. To show me my strength. My faith. My steadfast resolve in truth and purpose. And it's for the enemy, to show him that I am the Father's daughter, I will not stray, I will not curse, and I will not turn from my Holy Father. No matter what, God is my go-to.

When all of the previous tactics of the enemy failed, the devil still hadn't gotten wise to the authority provided in who I am created to be or the covering that I had in wielding that spiritual authority. My heavenly Father was standing right behind me with His arms crossed looking at the Devil saying, "I dare you."

The enemy dispatched the host of two thousand demons against me, Legion. And she was on her way.

In the biblical account of Legion, these particular demons add a considerable amount of strength and only bow to Jesus (and the Father), and just as in the Bible, demons, as a whole, are known to operate in familiar ways, territorial, and with repetition.

Legion was in the midst of her journey into town at that time. She was assigned to hurt, destroy, and derail me and my mission. Just like Jezebel.

As I reflected on previous days, I realized that while Doyle and I were going about our day of walking in the Spirit of the Lord everyday, the enemy's army was drawing closer, one step at a time. It was a reality that suddenly had clarity. I knew it from the scriptures but to live it was a different feeling. That evening, I remember my words before closing my eyes. Thinking about the enemy army marching forward toward me, I stated my position…"So be it," and drifted off to sleep.

The next day, Doyle and I followed our morning routine. Meet for prayer, grab breakfast, then jump into the mystery vehicle and head into the unknown.

By this point in our journey, we were so far past being surprised by anything that everything seemed normal, and we were ready at all times. So, it wasn't any surprise when my car door flew open as our vehicle rounded a corner. Our driver was driving a bit aggressively (more so than our normally aggressive drivers) that morning and taking corners faster than he probably should. Seat belts were not an option in many of the vehicles we were in and today was one of those days. When I say the door flew open, it wasn't just slightly ajar. The car door was completely open. It opened so suddenly and with such force that the door bounced on the hinges several times.

Here I was, just me and the door that was now open and the momentum of the turns keeping it open as I bounced around in the seat as a result of the unpaved, rock, and dirt road. But as always, God was larger than that. Regardless of the momentum, regardless of the bouncing or the lack of seatbelts, regardless of the fact we were still going around sharp corners, and regardless of the fact that the driver never slowed down or stopped, I felt firmly in place as if I was being held securely in position against the seat. I saw Doyle's movements out of the corner of my eye as he tried to get his arm passed me to the door, but he was bouncing around on the other side of the car.

Without any thought, I reached out, grabbed, and slammed the car door shut while we were still moving. I looked at my partner. He had kept trying to span the distance between us to secure me but once he saw that I was ok, he was ok.

He shook his head in astonishment and exhaled. He took my hand, and we were even more determined to see this through. "Thank you, Lord," were the words that came from Doyle as he squeezed my hand and then released.

People will not separate us in this mission, and neither will the spiritual. The enemy will not prevail. There is an anointing on this unity.

Really?!

Upon arrival at our drop off point, our interpreters were in the distance making their way toward Doyle and I as we said goodbye to the driver and jumped out of the vehicle.

Again, it was suggested and asked if we would be willing to split up, my partner going his own way and me going mine with our interpreters. I did my best not to openly laugh at the persistence trying to separate us. Really?!

These are the same interpreters we are with each and every day. Doyle taking one side of the village pathways and huts and I taking the other. It made no sense that these same interpreters who complemented the way we minister collectively and look out for each other were not giving up on trying to separate us into separate villages.

I turned to the sound of Doyle's voice as he said, "No, she and I remain together."

The interpreters looked at each other and spoke to each other in Swahili. Was there a hidden agenda?

Doyle further enforced what he was saying, "We remain in the same village at the same time. When we leave one village to head toward another, we leave the village together.

My interpreter was not giving up, "We could cover more ground if we split up," but Doyle was not having it.

Doyle put one figure up in front of him and spoke very clearly and with intention, "One village at a time." He motioned with that same finger back and forth between us as he continued, "She and I...same village." They wanted to discuss it more, but my partner shut it down. We had already been advised that the "white woman" was the talk of the town because I was the only white woman that some had ever seen in that area. We were also advised that kidnappings were normal in this village and that the witch doctor would love to meet the "white woman," so Doyle and I remained linked in solidarity.

There were other suspicious "offers" being made to me that would make some scratch their heads, such as when I was asked to sing on a record while I was there. He said, "It will be fun, and you can say you are on an African record." When I asked if Doyle would join, he said Doyle would not be allowed to attend or even know where it was…many things were very suspect. So, the clear answer was, "No." That discussion was also not over but again Doyle put a stop to that as well.

Bottom line, we will not be divided. Period!

About 10 minutes later, we arrived. As we walked through the village, we were almost immediately met with a woman. This woman was actually carrying a tree on her head. Not a twig, not a branch, but an actual tree. She looked to be 80 years of age and smiled from ear to ear. She seemed like a genuinely happy woman.

We stopped next to her, and she stopped walking in response. Through our interpreters we asked, "Excuse me, but how old are you?"

She considered the question for a moment and responded, "I don't know." When we asked how she was unaware of her age, she sweetly stood there with a tree on her head and explained birth was never recorded.

"Wow!" I immediately felt the freedom in not having the stigma of age on her. There was no countdown of decline. There was no chronological expectation of what she should or should not be doing. There is freedom in that. There is a different life waiting when we are walking in freedom and not conforming to society's standards.

"There is no one telling me I'm too old do this," she said.

Wow, we DO say these things to our people in America. "You're too old or your too young to understand, to carry that, to contribute." Yet this woman is free of all of that.

She went on to explain, "There is no one placing restrictions on me that my body disagrees with. There's no one to judge me based on age, because I have none."

She has no labels! She lives like most do in this place, without calendars or clocks. There are not work schedules because there is little work available except to eat and have shelter. They have no demands of stylish clothing or striving for social status. She is free. We proceeded past her and walked up to another compound.

This one, just like the other, had a large metal door with a grand pillared entrance. This one was so very different inside, but still had the barbed wire, razor wire, spiked fence, and locks on the gates, but the pink entryway and walls with all the greenery almost made it feel like a little oasis. We knocked on the door of this entryway and were met with a sweet young girl also dressed in bright pink. Like the other compound, she ran to get an older member of the family to ask permission for our entry. As we stood waiting at the gate, I looked around. Such a stark contrast. The varying shades of beautifully pink painted walls. The bright green well-manicured bushes and floral arrangements were so peaceful in comparison to the looped barbed wire that was mounted on top.

A young man named Alex came to the door and invited us in. We told him we were there in the name of Jesus. His reply was precise, "I know." He was very quiet and nodded without much of a word. He looked sad, without much expression. His head was not held up, but more of a downward gaze. He motioned for us to follow him as he asked us to come into his house. It was clear this young man was in need of hope and something that he lacked at the time.

Alex was Muslim and had many questions for Doyle and me. The depth of his desire to know the answer to his questions was evident. When hearing the answers, we watched as Alex considered what he heard. Without a word, he held out his hands to receive the prayer of Salvation. This young man felt the call.

We no more than said the word "Amen" and his face just glowed with renewal. He was elated at "this feeling inside." We explained it was the Holy Spirit and said our goodbyes.

"You knew I needed this exactly at that moment. God must have sent you."

We walked casually into a small courtyard that held a family of seven. When we walked in, they looked up and said hello in Swahili but not much of a smile on anyone's face. We told them we were there in the name of Jesus and asked them if we could speak with them for a moment. Without a word, one of the women walked past and retrieved something for us to sit on. No welcoming words, just a motion to sit and get down to business.

Immediately, we accepted the gesture and took a seat. The women remained silent for the most part, speaking only when we spoke to them directly.

The man spoke, "We are familiar with Jesus but do not know who Jesus was or why Jesus is so important."

The words were not filtered with kindness, instead very business-like. The atmosphere was rigid, borderline welcoming with no one moving. They sat quietly, without statement or real effort to communicate. My partner began speaking with the family as a whole, but I watched the motionless silent people.

I received in the spirit, "The man is the key." I recognized that the man in red was a powerful man. Both in the family and in the spiritual. "He needs to be validated," was clear in my spirit and that he was the key to the salvation of every member there.

I waited for my partner to finish what he was compelled to say, and as we do, he picked up on the moment that I was being instructed to speak on behalf of the Holy Spirit. I turned to the man in red and I spoke to him directly. We were eye to eye and without wavering. That is something that was not necessarily welcome from a woman here. At that moment, boldness was from the Holy Spirit, and I was choosing to let it move me, "Holy Spirit showed me you are a strong man. A man that people listen to when you speak."

Suddenly, the stone-cold set face began to crack into a softer version of himself. He acknowledged the accuracy of what Holy Spirit was telling him. He uncrossed his arms and leaned forward. He began to give several examples of people in the village that he guides.

I continued, "You have a responsibility over that gift. That gift to guide didn't come from you. It was given to you. You have a responsibility to teach people and guide them well. How do you do that without the God who gave you such a gift?" He nodded his head in approval and sat quietly in consideration.

The more we spoke, the more he softened. I continued to talk to him and told him biblical events, stories of the Bible, and the Gospel of the Good News. He became intrigued and said that he wanted to teach people about these same stories. I almost giggled because he was Muslim and was looking forward to talking about Jesus? Only God could do that.

"Before you talk about Jesus, do you want to experience him?" I asked.

He nodded in assurance that he did.

"Would you like to accept Jesus into your life and into your heart? Would you like to have Jesus as your Lord and Savior?"

After a few moments of silent consideration, he made the decision. "I do want to speak and teach others of Jesus and I want to know more." He stopped in consideration of his next words, "I do want to accept Jesus as my Lord and Savior."

It was in that very moment that the entire family moved. Each person stood up as we gathered in a circle, holding hands. It was in that moment that they followed the man's lead, and each person repeated the salvation prayer, accepting Jesus as their one and only God. All this took place as the littlest children crawled around our feet.

It was as if God Himself dropped into the center of this enclosed courtyard. An immediate change in the atmosphere was over us. Apprehension left and a flood of joy, peace, and smiles filled the void. Glory to God.

As we walked further, we literally wandered off the beaten path and toward a mud brick building that had my attention for some reason. We spotted three women sitting on a decorated bamboo mat. Two of them were preparing food.

We announced ourselves and that we were not a threat, but we again were not welcome. With grim faces, they said hello. I knew instantly I was called to minister to these women solo. The Lord had lit them up in the spirit and I was about to be shown the key.

"I'm here for a festival to speak about Jesus," I said.

"We know, but we are Muslim." They were cold but kept speaking to me. They were so dismissive I went straight to the Holy Spirit as I stood in front of them in silence. I received key information and I spoke it.

I bent over to try and get more equal with them in height because what I was about to say was going to have consequences, I just didn't know what kind. I turned to my interpreter and said, "I need you to translate this exactly as I say it." Without question, he nodded his head in acceptance and approval.

I turned to look at one particular woman and asked, "Have you ever noticed that you know things that you should not know?" As soon as I said those words and the translator translated them, the eyes of one of the women darted over to another woman with shock on her face.

I felt a shift in the spirit as the interpreter spoke the words to them. I asked again a new way, to make sure they understood the question. "Have you noticed that when your brain knows one thing, but your gut knows something more clearly. The gut, that feeling in here (I pointed to my sternum) doesn't match with what you know in your head?"

The interpreter spoke the words and they smiled. He said the women were in awe of this statement. The one I was directing the question to started to bob her head up and down in excitement. "Yes, yes, that just started this week! We didn't know what it was," she said.

I told them, "That is the Holy Spirit calling you to Him, showing you that He is with you." They began talking amongst themselves and invited us to sit down. The Lord had their attention. He told them something that they could not deny. God was loving them through me.

I continued to teach them about the love of Jesus. I asked them each what they knew about Jesus. They knew nothing, only that they were Muslim. It was then that the Lord gave me the rest of the information to convey. To the pregnant woman, I asked, "What do you want for the child in your stomach?"

When her eyes responded to the question, but she didn't have the language to express it, I continued. I asked her in another way. I pointed to the baby that another woman was holding. I said, "These children can grow up knowing the love of Jesus," and I asked one of the women, the same woman that indicated that she had been getting Holy Spirit clarity that week, if she wanted Jesus into her life.

She restated that she was Muslim and could not accept "this Jesus." I looked at a woman that was to her left, wearing a brightly colored striped dress, and asked, "What does your heart tell you?"

She sat quietly for a few moments in deep contemplation. No one said anything. This was her moment to listen to God her way. Then she raised her head and spoke the words, "Yes, I want to receive the prayer."

I walked over to get closer, "Can I come sit with you?"

She gave permission with a nod of her head.

"Will you hold out your hands?" Again, she complied as she looked at me with open anticipation.

As I looked her in the eyes and led her to Jesus in the prayer of Salvation, she said she felt strange. I explained to her that was the joy of Jesus and she started to giggle and laugh.

She instantly had joy where there was a sour face. I turned to the woman who originally said she did not want the prayer. I asked her again, "Do you want the prayer too?"

She responded, "The prayer you said with her was enough," indicating that she was making choices her way in her own timing.

I accepted that answer and asked Holy Spirit for the next direction. I was surprised to hear the response in my spirit. "If the prayer for her is enough, wouldn't you want the same, if not more, for your own touch from God?" She thought for a few minutes quietly. She looked at her hands. She sat quietly not saying anything. I was satisfied with her original reply, but God knew something I didn't, so I proceeded to wait.

After a few moments, then in a thoughtful tone said, "Yes, I want the prayer." I asked for permission to hold her hands. She gave it and began to repeat the prayer of Salvation after me to accept Jesus as her Lord and Savior.

We sat for a while and talked to the family. Before getting up, I looked at my interpreter. He had a strange un-telling look on his face.

"What's wrong?" I asked.

He just kept looking at me when he said, "This does not happen. What you bring is like Holy Spirit with us."

I laughed and watched as she began to laugh, and joy overflowed from her as well.

"It feels like He is here."

I nodded and exchanged nakupendas, hugs, blowing kisses to each of the family members. This was also something new that they had not seen before, love without borders.

"This is exactly what Jezebel was trying to stop," I thought to myself as we walked away.

As we left, they yelled out their promises to be at the festival to learn more about Jesus. We would have no idea if that would be the case because of the size of the crowds, but we believed their hearts desired to be there.

We had one more day of street ministry before our evening would be filled with the festival plans. It only seemed reasonable for manifestations to begin. However, it would have been nice to have a moment of rest between conflict, but that is not how the darkness behaves.

When a person or a team or a family is a threat, the attacks begin. As the person, team or family perseveres, the attacks often increase. Now one might make the same mistake as Job's friends did in the Bible and indicate that attacks are coming because that person did wrong, that the team was weak, or because that family is not right with God. However, there is a reason that the book of Job is in the Bible. That reason is to educate the spiritually immature away from those miss-teachings and those misunderstandings. You see, just as in the book of Job, God knew Job's strength and it was by His invitation that Job was put through the test. God knew Job would prevail because He knew Job's love for Him, but the enemy was cocky and prideful enough that he thought he could torment and attack Job to get the desired result. Along came Job's "friends" and each indicated that he brought such pain and heartache onto himself. However, it was the "friends" of Job that God was angered against for suggesting such a thing. God is never fooled by the Devil. He is never caught off guard. God is never chasing the Devil to ward off the enemy. God is in control. God allows or forbids all things. Including the attacks on me.

Not only did each attack bring me closer to my Heavenly Father, but He was teaching me through practical application just how far He will go to watch over me, protect me, and press forward on His own plans. I was His tool, and He was the hand that moved the tool. The enemy was lame enough to believe he could break this tool. The Devil was wrong. My Heavenly Father knew I would not break, and what the Devil meant for harm, my God used for good.

These spiritual atmospheric changes we were occurring with more intensity. It only made sense for the Hag to show up and make her debut.

The Festival

That evening, our car picked us up to take our place at the festival. We were asked to man the "prayer tent" which in reality was a full-fledged deliverance M.A.S.H. (Mobile Army Surgical Hospital) unit.

The Festival is a gathering of large crowds that come to celebrate, worship, and learn about Jesus. Crowds can swell from 60,000 – 150,000 people or more, depending on location. At each festival, there is a central location for the stage for singing, preaching, dancing, and speaking. To the left or right of the stage is a large tent or two, roughly 20x20. This tent was established for prayer and was generally filled with the lame, blind, and terminally ill that sat quietly waiting for prayer. Each person hungry for the healing power of Jesus. Others just wanted salvation and hope prayed over themselves and their families. This was how the prayer tent began. However, that would not last long. This same tent would later fill with the demonized and the manifesting.

Upon arrival, we were escorted through the crowd of many hundreds of people. People were peering in the windows of the vehicles, yelling hello and I love you while knocking on the vehicle as we creeped by. They were reaching toward us and waving. Our windows were down and as we proceeded through the crowd, many tried grabbing onto our hands or whatever they could reach.

It was a chaotic scene. A scene that was so loud that when we were in our own vehicle, the sheer volume penetrated the closed windows preventing us from speaking in normal tones. The sound system sounded like it was at max capacity, although I don't know if it was. We rolled down the windows and watched.

There was constant movement all around the vehicle as if celebrities had just come in town and everyone wanted to grab a photo or touch us. I had never seen anything like it in my life and probably never will again. The vehicle crept at a speed so slow through the crowd that it wasn't even registering on the speedometer.

It felt like we were more or less in a rapidly rolling vehicle rather than being driven.

The crowd was so thick it was difficult to identify individuals. They were just moving bodies everywhere, shoulder to shoulder, and each jockeying for attention.

It was then that two women caught Doyle's eye. He quickly motioned to them, but because of all the people pressing up against our vehicle, I could not originally see who it was he was referring to. I finally saw who he was pointing to. It was two of the three women who promised to attend. But the MOST surprising part of it was, they had taken off their Muslim head coverings and were openly saying Jesus while full of joy and blowing kisses to us.

God had done something amazing so quickly. There is nothing He can't do. The locals continued to be astounded as they repeated the phrase, "The number of people choosing Jesus is something we have never seen."

I will never forget the sight in front of me that first night we were escorted to the stage. Thousands of people were in all directions. We listened to the introduction and the presentation of the Gospel as we watched the people yell and jump in excitement at the name of Jesus.

That night was the festival introduction. It was the night the Hag was going to make herself known. Cocky, prideful, sarcastic, evil entities can never keep themselves quiet for too long, so it was only a matter of time before the ugliness gave itself a face.

After the festival, I went back to my bungalow to settle in for the night. We were all very tired and I personally just looked forward to a shower and to close my eyes for the night. I closed the door to my bathroom. I had taken my shower and suddenly felt the presence of another. I knew I was not alone. I felt what I could not see in the physical. I stared at the mirror over the sink, focusing my thoughts on what I was sensing. I turned off the water in the shower and focused on grabbing my water bottle to brush my teeth. I felt the presence get stronger. I knew I had locked the door to my bungalow. I heard no movement outside my door, but the presence was growing. I turned and faced the door to confront the intruder.

Flesh wrestled with spirit. "Did someone have a key to my door?" I wondered.

I stood there listening for a moment. I knew it felt sinister, but I wasn't about to give it any of my energy. I turned the water on after I brushed my teeth to wash off the toothpaste that I had gotten on my hand when I felt it move. The only sound was the sound of the running water as I worked to remain still.

I turned back to the running water, grabbed my towel, turned the water off and prepared to come out to a person. "Perhaps a team member or laundry lady," I speculated. I knew it felt sinister but based on what happened with Jezebel, anything seems possible at this point.

I opened the door and rounded the corner to my room. As I did so, I also walked directly into the gaze of a witch standing in the corner of my bungalow in full manifestation, not speaking, just glaring at me as if she was trying to see through me. She was angry. It was similar to looking at a ghost. She appeared to be a solid person yet at the same time…not.

Her hair was black and gray, aged by time. I don't remember anything else on her face to indicate age, but her eyes were deeply set and black around the orbital bone. She stood without any movement, perfectly still, staring at me.

Looking the Hag squarely in the face, the authority that moved throughout my body flowed outward in spoken word, "Get out. You are forbidden here."

Upon those simple words exiting my mouth, she immediately complied.

I let out a sigh of exhaustion from the day and crawled into bed. Once I was sure she was completely gone, I picked up my cell phone. I text Doyle, "A witch was in my room tonight. She's gone now. Stay alert. Good night." I sent a message to Janice via an app advising her of something similar and went to bed.

Sleep came easy that night. Whether it was exhaustion from the day or because I was going to need it didn't really matter. What mattered was I was resting. What I did not know was that the Hag would leave my room only to manifest in the room of another within a few seconds.

The next morning, as we gathered for breakfast as usual. Doyle asked me about the text and the entity I encountered.

"Well, she looked old. Her hair was grey and black, and her eyes were dark, deep."

"What was it?" He asked a bit more curious than normal.

"I don't know. I was so tired. I knew it was some kind of witch. That was all I cared about. Why?"

Doyle wasn't satisfied with that answer, so he probed deeper, "I need you to ask the Lord what that was."

This was not like Doyle, so I did as he desired. I asked.

Sitting quietly, I took a moment to check in with the Lord and got an immediate response. "A Hag."

Doyle, still not satisfied, continued, "So, what is that? What does it mean?"

Something was up with Doyle, and he was not ready to tell me what it was yet, so rather than just dropping the subject, I began looking it up.

I was stunned when I found it. I showed Doyle my findings right there in black and white. Doyle seemed intrigued yet somewhat satisfied, nodding his approval.

What my partner and I didn't know was the impact that Hag was to have later on the lead Evangelist and my partner. What I didn't know was why Doyle was so interested in this particular entity, but there would be an added element of confirmation and completion to come.

Day 1

Doyle and I knew we needed to be at the festival before it started. Our arrival time was around three o'clock when the others would also begin to trickle in. Knowing this, Doyle and I took to the villages of Songea again, and this time we were joined by my sweet friend, Danielle. She and I were back on solid footing with each other. God gave me the grace to forgive and her the humility to ask for forgiveness.

After being dropped off, we began our trek into and through the villages. Again, as per custom, our interpreters took us by the hand as we began another day of spreading the name of Jesus. There were three of us and only two interpreters, so once we were in the villages, Doyle and I ventured to separate areas of the same village. I went out on my own with my interpreter, while Danielle chose to go with Doyle and his interpreter. It was kind of weird not having my partner by my side, but I knew that Jesus was large and in charge of all that occurred, so we continued going from place to place speaking the Gospel and offering the name of Jesus to those who wanted to hear about Him.

I wandered into an area where children were sitting on a slab of concrete in front of a house. The children were so small. I asked, "Where's your mom?"

Without a word, they pointed us around the corner and down a narrow rock filled dirt path that led to a handmade dirt step that was 2 feet off the ground, which led into a courtyard between several clay and concrete houses. The pathway was so confining, and the ground was so unsteady that I used my left hand to follow the wall of the mud houses and my right hand against rocks and dirt hillside to keep myself balanced and my footing in place. We came to the end of this tunnel like path and there was only one way left to go...up.

Sizing up this two-foot step made of dried dirt and straw I wondered, "Ok, how am I going to do this?" Shrugging my shoulders and looking at my interpreter, I lifted my skirt up and hoisted myself onto this crumbling mound of dirt. It was as uneven as the pathway was.

As I continued to climb, I thought to myself, "Perhaps this was where water drained into or through during the rainy season." Every surface was water and wind worn. Just to stay upright, there was no choice but to use the walls to bounce off. Even my interpreter was bouncing off the adjacent dirt walls. "Oh good, it wasn't just me," I thought to myself

As we rounded a corner from the narrow corridor, the area suddenly opened into a courtyard where a male and two females sat on a concrete or rock ledge. There was no furniture, no doors, and no curtains. Only openings into their abode. Ironically, one of the women held a cell phone.

We came upon them so suddenly that they didn't even have time to fake their welcoming faces, so I began to open the dialogue. "Hello, how are you?" They did not respond, so I continued, "I'm here to spread the name of Jesus." Looking at the woman who was holding a phone I asked her, "Do you know who Jesus is?"

She confirmed that she did but was making her position known that she was not interested in any additional dialogue as she immediately looked back down at her phone. She was actively trying to dismiss me.

I asked the Lord a quick, "Do I stay, or do I leave?"

I received, "Stay," so that was what I was going to do. Once I knew that I was to stay, I found her dismissal amusing because I knew it wasn't going to stay that way for long.

Turning my attention to the woman who was sitting in the chair across from the woman with the phone, I asked her, "Do you know Jesus?"

Immediately, she replied, "No, please tell me."

I wondered to myself how can these two live in such close proximity, and one not tell the other of the Father of the Universe?

Without hesitation I began to tell the story of the "Good News" and gave her a word from God.

As I began sharing testimonies of how Jesus impacted my life, the woman with the cell phone was now completely engaged. She actually wanted to tell her stories of how Jesus impacted her life as well. It was then that the woman with the cell phone lifted her gaze completely from the dismissive uninterested position to almost glowing. She was excited as she joined me in talking about Jesus. She looked at me and leaned forward from her bench or rock and said, "Because I have Jesus, now my life is fuller, and I have peace."

As soon as she spoke those words, the woman in the chair spoke with both anticipation and anxiousness, "Yes, I want this Jesus too!"

I smiled as I considered what just occurred. This cold, unwelcoming woman just led her own friend to Jesus. "Unbelievable," I thought to myself.

Accommodating this fine young lady, I began to lead her in a prayer of salvation. She repeated word for word what I said and began raising her hands. She wanted to praise her Jesus now that she knew who He was.

I looked at the woman with the cell phone, "You have a responsibility to teach your friend about Jesus. You know Him. You have testimony and stories about how Jesus has changed your life. You must share what you know about Jesus with her."

She looked at me with a smile and excitement. It was then that I realized she just needed permission to speak of Him. I had forgotten we were in a Muslim village, so I clarified. "When it's safe, you speak truth, hope, and love of Jesus to her and let Jesus move inside your life. The Lord will protect you."

What was a cold, unwelcoming beginning, turned into a warm, heartfelt, joyful, praise-filled moment with God.

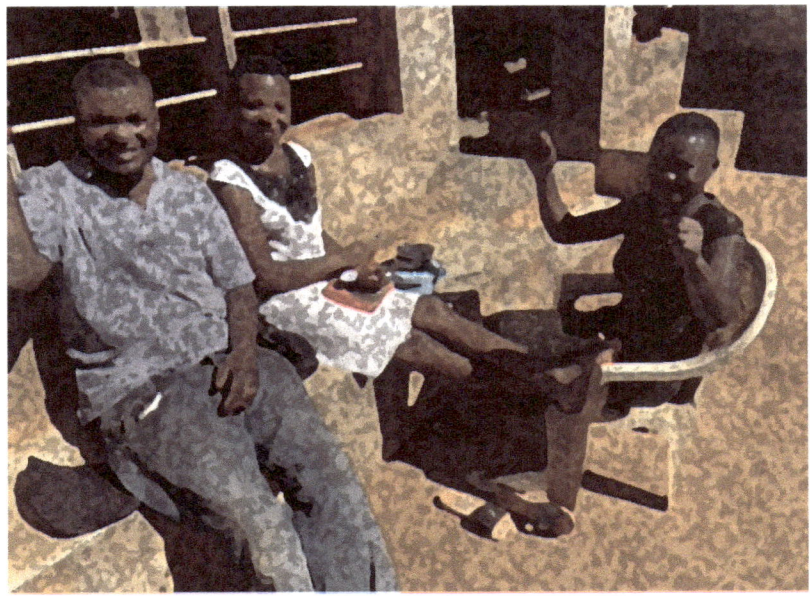

Step after step, God went before us and opened doors that seemed impossible and made them more than possible. Again, my interpreter was astonished as to what was happening. He had just one question as he turned to look at me, "How?" My reply was simple, "The Holy Spirit leads, and God does the work. We just follow."

He shook his head and was so focused on what just occurred that we were almost down the rickety pathway before he spoke. "I forgot to say to them Goodbye." I smiled. He was being personally affected.

We left the courtyard with his thoughts spinning and noticed a large group of children mingling around. Every now and again we would notice that we were being followed, but by now I was used to it. Little glimpses of heads popping out from beyond walls, rocks, trees, and between huts was now the norm, but these were now children doing the same.

Children of all ages had seen us walking around and through villages for days, occasionally waving just to dart behind something with a giggle that could be heard from a distance. The excitement in their eyes couldn't be contained. There was intrigue, curiosity, and a willingness to hear what we were there to say. Some would touch my skin to see if my white skin would rub off. Others put their hands against mine and compare with innocent questions of why I was different.

Doyle saw that the kids wanted to play, so he began to dance by making silly dance moves and encouraging them to mimic him, which they did so quickly and willingly. Other times, he pretended to chase them for a few steps, while they giggled and scattered only to come back for more. The smaller children would hold my hands or take handfuls of my skirt into their hands or arms and just look up at me with the biggest most beautiful eyes waiting for some kind of response. The children followed us everywhere we went, sometimes holding onto us, other times running behind us or in front of us. Life was sweet as we listened to and participated in the atmosphere, the laughter, and joy of the children.

As we made our way through the villiage, we stumbled upon a man on a bike. Doyle spoke to him while I stopped and spoke to an older man wearing a black shirt and a younger man wearing a green shirt down the road.

"We're Muslim," they announced, indicating that they knew exactly who we were.

At the sound of their voice, the three of us were joined by a woman lingering in the area. She wore green head wrap and scarf.

This was their winter season, so it was normal to see the people of Africa wearing winter coats, hats, and a scarf all at once in the eighty-degree weather we were experiencing.

I could see that the older gentleman was a very deep thinker. There was a depth to his spirit and a kindness in his heart. "Hello, I'm here as a representative of Jesus and teaching of His Good News for us all. Have you heard the Good News?"

That wording got is attention. "No, I want to know, what is the Good News?"

I responded, "The Good News I'm talking about is the news of Jesus Christ and what He did on the cross of crucifixion. Do you know of that good story?"

He shook his head. "No, tell me of Jesus," he replied.

We stood there talking openly about the life, death, resurrection of Jesus and the promises and loving hope of the

Lord as the woman in the scarf and head wrap milled around lurking with both intrigue and disgust.

He asked, "How do I get to serve this Jesus?"

Before I could answer his question, the woman in the green hat became visibly agitated. She had heard his question to me, and she was angry. "Is she Muslim?" I asked and motioned to her.

He confirmed that she was and with that she made herself scarce, quickly turning to walk away with a curse under her breath.

I turned back to him to answer his question. "If you wish to serve Jesus Christ, you must truly want Him as part of your life. To learn about Him and to love Him greatly. No other gods before Him. He is the only God that will save you with hope."

He considered my words for quite some time then asked, "What must I do?"

"Do you believe that Lord Jesus could love you enough to die for you?" I asked.

He thought for a moment. "No man can do this for another, but a God could do this, so yes," he said. He went on to express his understanding of the process, "This God Jesus was dead and then He came back to life?"

I smiled and said, "Yes, Jesus is a true God. He has mastery over death and life. Nothing can stop Jesus from His plans, and nothing can stop our God from His plans."

It was then that the woman reappeared and began hovering around us again. Each time I looked over, she had gotten closer in proximity and continued to advance ever so slowly.

He stood there considering what I had just said and then asked, "Where did you learn about this Jesus?"

"It's a book that's called the Bible. It's written so we can know the stories of this Jesus, so we can tell everyone of His goodness."

He thought for another long moment, and I remained silent and still so not to distract him as he wrestled with his thoughts. This was his journey. It's not my job to talk him into accepting Jesus or adopting any beliefs. I was just there to deliver the message.

Suddenly, his face cleared of any contemplation, "Yes, I want the prayer of Jesus."

The moment that came out of his mouth, the woman in the green hat had a visceral response. She physically backed away from us, holding my gaze. She kept moving backwards to put as much distance between her and I as she could. She just wouldn't or couldn't look away. Her eyes were glued to us as he spoke the prayer of Jesus one sentence at a time after me. She shifted her attention to the others and then began to slowly walk away as if almost afraid to move. I knew in my spirit she was going to go "get help" from the village elders but I refused to let her departure deter me from my assignment from God.

As she continued to back away and started to turn and run, I spoke, "I love you."

She stopped in her tracks and said with a smile that was never present before, "I love you too."

As soon as the words were out of her mouth, she looked shocked, but only for a moment. Her face then glowed with a smile as I turned my attention back to the men.

I called Doyle over and asked that he assist in leading the younger man in prayer. I took the hands of the younger man (mid-twenties to early thirties) as Doyle spoke the words to be translated. This young man locked eyes with me and never looked away. The entire prayer was spoken with such a loving look of desperation in his eyes I could almost swear he never blinked. We made a connection. There may have been a language barrier, but while the interpreter translated the words for him to repeat, the real language spoken was through the eyes of the man. He wasn't just looking at me, he was looking into me, and I was looking into him. The look on his face as we encouraged him to seek Jesus more was precious.

As we walked away, Doyle and I separated again. Danielle and Doyle went one direction, and my interpreter and I headed into another. My interpreter looked at me and said, "I thought you two would not be separated? Why now?"

I laughed and replied, "Danielle chose to go with him. I guess he figures I'm fine now." And I was. I was navigating this process alone and let the Lord lead.

I walked up to another house made of clay and tin. There was a man leaning against a wall. He stood up when I walked in and smiled so big that I had to wonder what was up.

He immediately began to speak, "I had seen you enter the village and have been excited to meet you."

"Why are you excited to meet me?" I asked

His response even surprised me, "I knew that God had sent someone to give me news."

Caught off guard I replied, "Can you explain that to me?"

He was all too happy to oblige, "Before you came, long ago I worked with tourists. I learned a lot through those tourists, and I discovered that there was a lot I did not know." He went on to say that he discovered that he could learn from people outside of the world he lived in.

Understanding what it was that he was conveying, I informed him I was there as a representative of the one and only Lord Jesus and to tell about His life, death, and resurrection.

His reply was immediate, "I'm Muslim," as he began to walk away.

Instantly, I heard in my spirit the words, "Tell him about freedom."

Quickly, before he could get any farther away, I began to tell him about the freedom that the blood of Jesus brought through His sacrifice. He stopped in his tracks and turned toward me. He was halfway across the courtyard as he crossed his arms and began to listen. I seized the moment and just began talking about Jesus and the Gospel. As I finished, I asked him what he thought.

"I need to meditate about it."

Smiling, I said, "Ok" and made some small talk while I waited to see Doyle and Danielle so I could join them.

"You're welcome to wait here if you like," He offered.

Looking at him one more time, I weighed my option and said, "Thank you, but I'm leaving now. My friend, I'm offering one more time to pray with you to ask Jesus into your life before I go."

There was a long silence as he looked at the ground with his arms crossed. Suddenly, he broke the silence with a nod of the head. I asked my interpreter to inquire as to what he was agreeing to. The man said, "I am ready to accept this Jesus as mine."

I asked if I could take his hands. He simply uncrossed his arms and said, "Yes." He repeated after me in accepting Jesus, however, because he was struggling with learning more about Jesus, we moved the prayer into what Jesus could do for his spiritual heart and his desires for hope. He began to get fidgety, but the smile on his face grew. Not knowing what was going on, I asked my interpreter what was up.

"Something in my chest feels warm and light," he replied. "I can't stop smiling. What is happening to me?"

I explained that was Holy Spirit moving within him, igniting and connecting Him to God.

He smiled even bigger and without notice, he grabbed me up in his arms for a long jovial hug. "Thank you for telling me about Jesus."

"You are very welcome my brother, God bless," and I walked out of the man's courtyard.

My interpreter asked me to keep going, "There are many more souls to save," he said, but I wasn't going any farther without Doyle. My interpreter was getting frustrated with me, urging me to keep walking, but I stood my ground, "I'm waiting for Doyle."

"He went with the other lady. They may not be seen for a while," he said trying to persuade me.

"I'll wait," were the only two words that came out of my mouth as I turned to look around for him. Off in the distance, I spotted Danielle surrounded by a lot of children. I joined them and started talking to the children. It was then that Danielle got my attention and pointed to a woman outside of my line of sight. I looked into the direction she indicated and saw that there was a woman on the ground.

"Go see her," she said as she continued to point.

Danielle was right, this woman was indeed in bad shape, beyond depression.

"Hello."

She didn't move.

"Can I sit with you?" I asked.

Again, she didn't move. I decided to take my place sitting next to her. "Did you know that the Holy Spirit doesn't want you to feel so heavy and sad?"

She lifted her head from her down cast gaze. Something about her cried out to me. I looked around and noticed that we were sitting amongst the tall stalks of the local crop. She was trying to hide from life. Her eyes went from holding my gaze to dropping to the ground as she said, "I'm Muslim."

"I understand. Can I tell you a story?" I asked.

She kept her face pointed toward the ground she was sitting on as she spoke, "Yes."

Moving forward, I told her of the life, death, and resurrection of my precious Jesus. "Would you like Jesus in your life?"

Turning her head and raising her face, she just stared at me without a word for a long time. Her eyes deep with sadness. When she spoke, it made my heart cry out for freedom on her behalf, as she repeated, "I can't. I'm Muslim."

Accepting what she said at face value, I continued building a trust between us. "Did you know that Jesus is sad because you are so sad?" I saw something come across her face that I could not identify. "Did you know that Holy Spirit wants to lift your pain off of you?"

Through the interpreter, she said, "Tell me about the pain He wants to lift." That was a crack in the wall that she was holding between us.

I told her I was a representative of Jesus and the Kingdom of Heaven in the name of Jesus. "Watch this." I raised my hand to her arm and said the name above all names. It only took once before she got to witness His power.

"Jesus."

She broke out in uncontrollable laughter, belly rolling, leaning forward and then backward. She couldn't stop she was so full of joy, and I had the privilege of watching as Jesus' presence took authority over the woman's pain and despair.

As I removed my hand, the laughter immediately stopped. She asked me in confusion, "What was that?"

"That was the Holy Spirit. The spirit of the Lord I serve." She looked at me inquisitively. I explained that Jesus sent the Holy Spirit to us and that the presence of God and Jesus is within that Holy Spirit. That was the simplest way to teach something so complex as the trinity in a field of dead crops. Doing my best to break it down as cleanly as possible so that she could understand the magnitude of what she just experienced, I showed her one more time. This time I spoke in her language. I touched her arm again as I said the name that mattered, "Yesu."

As soon as I touched her, she broke out again in uncontrollable laughter. I sat with my hand on her arm for a few minutes letting her soak in what was occurring and enjoy a few moments of peace and joy. When I removed my hand, the laughter left her like the faucet just turned off. She looked at me confused.

I explained to her what just occurred with more detail. "As God's representative, the power of the Holy Spirit flows through me and that was the part of Him that you felt."

She was astounded and looked as if she wanted more. As I spoke to her more about Jesus, I saw that it was almost time for us to get moving again. I offered her the prayer of Salvation one last time. She sat there for a few moments looking at the ground. I could see that she wanted to accept, but self-condemnation was all over her.

Her words said it all, "I cannot accept the prayer." It wasn't that she didn't want to, but she wasn't allowed to, and her fear was abundant.

Seeing that she was so clearly torn, I did what God instructed. "Did you know you can accept Jesus even after I leave?"

Her eyes were suddenly full of interest as she glanced around searching for something or someone.

"You don't need me to accept Jesus. You just need to talk to God in private." She was fully engaged again. "When you feel safe, secure and ready to surrender the pain in your life to Jesus, ask Him to be your Lord and savior."

She just looked at me with wide eyes, glancing around as if she knew she was doing something that was going to get her in trouble.

"You are safe. You are covered right now," I assured her. "When you feel in your spirit you want to answer that feeling inside of you to believe in Jesus, the cross, and Jesus coming back from death, you can pray to Him."

She continued to listen intently as if there was no one else around us. I felt in my spirit, "She wants to repent." I continued as instructed from the Lord. "When you are ready to ask Him for forgiveness, you can pray to Him." I didn't know what she needed forgiveness for, but it wasn't my business. It was between her and God. "When you want to be free of the other gods and ready to love just the One God, you can pray to Him."

Suddenly aware that we were not alone, and she was probably being watched, she nodded quickly while assessing her surroundings. Quietly, she spoke, "Thank you. I love you," in her native language.

Assuring her I loved her as well, I got up and joined Doyle and Danielle. By then the crowd dissipated and it was time to move on. As I began to walk, children's hands appeared in mine and the hands of Doyle. They were skipping and bouncing, giggling, and laughing as they lead us through the dirt roads in their village. We wove in and out of the footpaths and in between huts. Those children let go of my hands and ran ahead while two smaller children, around kindergarten age, took their place by my side.

Their little hands were so small in mine, but they could not contain their curiosity and their excitement as they walked me, practically dragged me, to their homes with a dozen other children following behind.

Laughter was pouring from my lungs as these little bitty children were doing their best to hurry me and other members of our team. Soaking in the sounds of little children all around me was almost surreal. "Could life really be this free and easy?" I wondered. The giggles continued as the children and our team climbed up, jumped over, and stepped around the obstacles on the footpaths.

The children led me up to a woman cooking bananas in a huge open pan. As I approached with the children on either side of me and their hands in mine, I said, "Hello," in Swahili. I turned around and noticed that Doyle and his interpreter had walked on to another location.

The woman straightened to a standing position from the open pan she was bending over. Without hesitation, the woman spoke, "What good news do you bring to us today?"

I couldn't believe how welcoming this woman was. I could not contain my laughter as I responded, "The joy of the Good News of Jesus."

She smiled and without hesitation said, "I know Him. He lives inside of me."

With those simple words, we both broke out into a celebratory laughter with clapping of hands in a conveyance of joy in our excitement. We spoke for a few moments and blew each other a kiss good-bye.

Without a moment's notice the children grabbed back onto my hands and escorted me to the next hut. We approached a house with a woman sitting out front. I looked at Danielle, "This lady is yours."

She nodded as I took a moment to myself and watched from the sidelines. I was all too happy to play with the children while she led this wonderful lady to Jesus.

I heard a sound that didn't fit the occasion that jolted my attention away from the children and over to Danielle. A man came out, clearly unaware that the woman he was yelling at, to, or about was not alone. He was yelling something in Swahili. However, he abruptly stopped when he realized we were there. He was drunk. He immediately changed his demeanor and invited us in. As he placed his hand on my back to escort us in, I moved backward away from the doorway. My thoughts were, "Let's see…An angry drunk man in a Muslim village…um yep, we can stay out here."

The man repeated the same behaviors with Doyle. Doyle informed him that we were grateful for his invitation but wanted to talk to him outside. The man wasn't just drunk, he was sloppy drunk. Looking at Doyle, I smiled, "This one is for you."

As Doyle began talking to him about the reason we were there, the man became resistant. We were preparing to leave when, without warning, the man said in his native language, "I'm Muslim, but it's not working out for me." Those were his actual words as spoken through our translator. The man continued, "I have read some of the Bible." To prove he had indeed read it, he began to recite portions of scripture in his drunken state. He continued to recite scripture after scripture and as he did, he became more and more sober. I couldn't help but smile. He wasn't stone cold sober but definitely better than he was.

In that sobriety, he began to get inquisitive. "I have questions for you."

Doyle gave him his full attention.

"Some of the scriptures say that a man can have more than one wife. Why?"

Doyle answered his question gracefully as always.

The man began to go through various other scriptures asking for understanding of the meaning of each because he truly wanted to know yet was clearly struggling. He started to bargain with Doyle, "I will accept Jesus if you will put me through Bible school. I want to preach."

Smiling, Doyle responded, "You need to have something to preach if you want to preach."

The Holy Spirit in me lit up in that moment and I knew it was my time to engage this man. "Excuse me, preaching is not what you know. It's a matter of faith."

He looked at me for a long while. His hands still suspended in midair in the former gesture he shared with Doyle. He didn't move and his mouth was still open. As I looked at him, I was discerning how much of the stare was alcohol and how much was internal conviction or "the call."

As if to jolt him into awareness, I repeated myself, "It's not what you know. It's a matter of faith. Would you like to know *about* Jesus, or would you like to have Jesus in your life?"

That statement resulted in another stare.

"It's important to know about Him in the Bible, but it's more important to want Jesus in your heart and to want to love him."

He dropped his head in consideration of what was said. "You are right. I want him in my heart."

Doyle stepped back into the conversation at that point and led him to Jesus.

"Do you have a Bible that I can read?"

Doyle responded, "I'm sorry but we don't have any Bibles to give to the people." However, God had a plan for that as well.

As we began to head out of the village for the day, the number of children following us had multiplied substantially. They stayed as close to us as possible, following us all the way through the village to the main road/pathway. As we turned around to wave goodbye to all those who were trailing us, we watched each bounce up and down in excitement, waving and blowing kisses as they turned around and ran back to their village.

We proceeded to our pickup point to return to the bungalows for a quick rest before the festival. That afternoon, as we gathered in the dining area, a team member brought three Bibles. I remember looking at the stack of Bibles on the table and saying, "I wish we had a few of those for our outreach."

Someone at the table responded, "Are they needed?"

Doyle responded, "If I only had one earlier today, it would have been helpful." With that simple dialogue, Doyle received three to put into his backpack and it would be needed.

Spirit of Suicide Expelled

Full Impact Exposed

That evening, as we gathered at the at the "prayer tent," I was so excited to see my interpreter that had been with me in the streets pop up out of the already forming crowd. I jumped up and down with excitement that he would be my interpreter again. We didn't have any assigned to us and were not sure how we would be able to minister that evening, but God provided...again!

My interpreter was excited as he told me he had an update for me.

"What is it?" I asked.

"Do you remember..." (He described a woman that we had prayed for early in the journey.)

"Yes! I remember her," I responded.

"She was contemplating suicide until you came."

I was on pins and needles waiting for the rest of what he had to say. This young lady did not tell me she was feeling or contemplating such a thing. She did not verbalize anything. I was completely unaware. But God wasn't unaware, God knew she was suffering.

"How is she?" I asked.

"She said that the spirit of suicide had been harassing her, plaguing her, and even pushing her into compliance. She went on to say that once she received the prayer in the name of Jesus, the spirit went away."

"Yes! That is all God!"

"Yes, but prophetess, she said the Holy Spirit filled her after the spirit left, that is not normal."

I couldn't help but laugh a laugh of joy. "It may not seem normal by religious standards, but it is exactly as it was intended to be. Please keep me posted"

NOTE: Once I was stateside, I was told that she was still doing well with the freedom of Jesus and the suicidal thoughts are no longer part of her life.

We were advised that we would be on the stage for part of the service and then retire into the prayer tent to serve the community. As a result, we began to move into place.

The service was amazing. The crowds were in the hundreds if not thousands, and everyone was engaged.

My partner got up partially through the stage introductions and headed for the prayer tent to serve and I was quick to follow. It was then that I was stopped by Ashby and asked to stay on the stage. He assigned me to the stage to observe what may not be clear to the natural or naked eye. He wanted to know how to pray the best and the method of spiritual attack. Engaging my spiritual instincts, I asked the Lord, "Show me what You want me to see." Within moments, as I looked out over the center of the crowd, I saw an entity. It took me a moment to fully understand what I was seeing. I felt my lips purse at the audacity of what I was seeing. It was the same witch that was in my room. She was there to rob, confuse, interfere, and oppress. This was unacceptable.

The people, regardless of age, were standing shoulder to shoulder, staring and waiting with anticipation on their faces. Children were climbing trees to see and hear the word of God spoken and preached. Children shook those same trees in dance and praise as they bounced up and down on the branches. It was quite a sight to see the trees moving in rhythm to the music and the Hag was hovering just above their heads.

On the stage, there was movement, song, dance, and people talking in my ear to interpret what was being said over the loud speakers. The stage was made of nothing more than scaffolding and thin wood planks that were bending and flexing with every step. There were over a dozen (closer to twenty-five) of us on the plank covered scaffolding before the dancing entertainers. The contraption that suspended us shook with every step or dance move causing our chairs to bounce while we were in them. The entire scene was captivating.

We had been told by officials to vacate the area before dark for our safety and to honor the time allotted by permit. Ironically, at no time, surrounded by thousands of people did I ever feel unsafe. Feeling very much at home, I silently giggled as I watched a single "soldier," carrying a long rifle that looked like it was right out of the civil war. He walked the line in front of the crowd, back and forth in effort to convey our "protection."

The lateness of the hour and the fluidity of the evening and atmosphere left me guessing as to what to expect minute to minute. It was almost dusk when we got the signal to go. As quickly as possible, we descended the stairs from the platform and began making our way back to the waiting cars through the crowd of people.

Someone strung string between the stage and the waiting vehicles in an effort to keep people back and our people together. Initially, my thoughts were, "How nice to have a clear path," but that thought didn't last long. As we walked, people two and three deep grabbed on to my arms, hands, my shoulder, or dress, touching wherever they could reach.

For every step I took, another three or four hands would reach out in desperation. Touching as many hands as possible, we kept moving. That contact meant something. My heart was aching to touch the hearts of everyone one in the crowd, but I knew it was impossible. That contact had purpose and God would do something with it. The hunger was so clearly there. The desire to know more about what we brought was front and center to all things. Hope was in the air.

Because I was on the stage and Doyle was in the prayer tent, I couldn't see him. All I could see or feel was the darkness of the night descending upon us and the many hundreds of hands reaching out to touch my body. Hearing was not an option because the speakers were still playing music for the performers on stage and the yelling of the people in their efforts to get our attention.

I walked where the string barrier led.

There was such a flurry of activity, there was no way of knowing where we were going at any time. There were cars waiting but no way of knowing which vehicle I was to get into versus the vehicles of others at the event. I felt hands on my back from a gentleman I trusted right behind me. The vehicles were filling up and we were all split up with the great deal of activity.

A vehicle slowly crept through the crowded mass of hundreds of people, and I jumped in waiting for any sign of Doyle. There was no Doyle to be seen in any direction I looked. The driver saw me looking around and before I said anything to the driver, he conveyed his concern, "We must go. We cannot wait." Looking out the back window, I watched as the crowd of people began to fill in the vacancy of where the vehicle just departed from. Many began to follow the vehicle with arms waving and smiles from ear to ear.

Turning back around to face the driver, I trusted I was in the right vehicle since I had no interpreter. This was not one of our regular drivers. He didn't look familiar at all. There was no real way of knowing if I was in a vehicle that was assigned to our team or just a vehicle that was brought into the area. Trusting in God, I waited for the car to pull up at the bungalows…at least I hoped it would.

As the first few people made it back, we were all asked to meet in Mike's room while waiting for the rest of the team to arrive. In doing so, we began talking about our experiences.

"The witch that was in my room was hovering above the crowd with tentacles that were touching the heads of many people in the crowd."

The lead Evangelist thought for a moment before confirming that he felt that same disruption during the same prayer time I saw the witch. At that time, he could not pinpoint it.

Flashbacks

The next morning at breakfast, I felt compelled to draw what I had seen the evening before. The witch, known as the Hag. I sat at the breakfast table scribbling it out quickly before it left my memory.

Doyle looked at it once, twice, and then took it from me and just stared at it. He didn't say anything to me about it. He just looked at it.

"Sorry, I'm not an artist. These are the best scribbles I can do."

Still, he said nothing.

The day went on as it had in past days when he said to me, "I've been thinking of the drawing you did at the table at breakfast."

I turned and looked at him, "You have? Why?"

He went on to explain the urgency that he expressed in finding out the name of the witch and seeing the drawing I made was the same entity he had personally experienced as a child. "It even behaved the same way you described." He went on to tell me his experience. "I recall standing on the back seat floorboards of my dad's car behind the driver's seat. My dad drove as I looked out and through the back window. We were traveling through a desert like landscape and there was a local geyser that went off. As this geyser blew, the witch you described and drew came out of the ground with it. I knew it was watching me intently."

I asked him, "Was it after you?"

"No, but I saw it and it was 'aware' of me. Very aware." He shook his head for a moment before continuing, "I had forgotten about her until you described her, and I saw the drawing."

"Interesting," I thought to myself. There are not an endless number of demons or evil spirits. Their army is not exponential. Instead, it's relatively finite in comparison to the army of angelic and the Kingdom. When the army is finite or small, you begin to run into the same spirits over and over. This time was no exception.

With that piece of information, Doyle and I turned our attention back to villages of Songea. That morning, when we were dropped off at our destination, there was a man waiting in front of a church dressed in traditional Muslim attire. He was holding a large stick that served as his cane and his protection. We sat down with him while we waited for our interpreters to arrive.

Doyle and I became comfortable enough with the village and some of the native language, so much so that we were openly engaging people as needed without the aid of interpreters. The man pointed downward toward his foot. It was then that we noticed his toes on his right foot were missing. They had been there, but they either rotted off or were cut off. To this day I'm unsure if leprosy was involved or not.

He asked for prayer and explained that he had come to the church asking for food or money for food. By this time, our interpreters arrived and indicated that they gave him some shillings during a previous encounter. We explained, "We don't carry any money, but if you like we could talk to you about Jesus and let Jesus be your provider."

Surprisingly, he agreed. As we spoke to him about the journey with Jesus, he listened intently, holding our eye contact, and nodding in understanding after the interpreters spoke. He seemed to carefully consider all that was said. He weighed every word. We were witnessing what was clear wisdom at work. He sat for a moment in deep silent consideration. He refocused from that place of pondering to direct eye contact again and began asking questions about Jesus. "What can Jesus do for me and my life now? And at my age?"

Doyle and I looked at each other and spoke the truths of who Jesus was and is. We continued to answer questions and let him know that he was loved by Jesus, and we loved him as well.

After a few moments, we told him, "We must go now. Do you want Jesus to be part of your life?"

He thought for a few more moments and said in a haggard and deep voice, "I'm tired of living the life I'm living. I want a life of peace with Jesus."

This man was full of surprises and the Lord was too. As he repeated the prayer, accepting Jesus as his Lord and Savior, he began to smile. "I have laughter again. I have joy…why?" The troubles he had when he arrived at the church still existed, but now there was peace and joy in the midst of it. He thanked us profusely as we said our goodbyes and began walking toward another village.

As we walked, I began to feel the spiritual weight increasing. "Uh oh," I said aloud. It would be closely akin to when you walk into a room full of people and you don't know what occurred before you walked in, but the tension was thick. I felt the hair on the back of my neck stand up, something was amiss. "Ok Lord, I feel the warning. Cover us."

The Shift

We didn't know it, but we had just walked into thick enemy territory with a witch doctor covering this village. He knew we were there. This force was strong.

I needed to warn Doyle, but I needed to be subtle about it because with a force this strong, I knew all to well how quickly the unarmored people of God can be influenced and turn against you. As we walked, I leaned over to my partner. "There's a lot of oppression in this area." I needed him to confirm what I was feeling. I needed my partner to have my back as I had his.

Instead, I got a dismissive remark, "So, what are you going to do about it? We just keep going."

Uh oh, my partner was affected. It happened just that fast. Doyle was not my partner in these moments. I was alone. The loving, unified partner that I've known for years was present but missing. Doyle was right there but suddenly I felt alone and isolated.

The aggression was building in the spirit and now I was responding in the flesh. Doyle had abandoned me. I was angry, in a foreign land, surrounded by witchcraft, not knowing where I was in this village, with no vehicle to leave in, and looking at people who were looking to me for guidance. How could my partner fall prey to this? How could I allow myself to respond with anger? This made for a very bad circumstance. I needed him by my side, but at that moment I was alone and ready for battle. I recognized the momentum of what was occurring in the spirit and a disdain in the spiritual realm.

One more time I tried to connect with my partner and when I got a similar response, I decided that was it. I was going to deal with this now. When I get quiet, something is up. And I got very quiet. My partner noticed I was different but what he didn't know was I was digging deep. Digging deep into my Jesus. Digging deep to fight against the flesh. Digging deep to re-center myself in the spiritual. I needed to go deep to override what was CLEARLY around me. Battling alone in the spiritual realm, I needed my partner, but he could not "hear" me. Doyle was pushing me away.

I Told You So...

Walking back, we encountered several women and children sitting outside on a porch. The moment they saw us they began to run and get wooden stools for us to sit on. It was as if they were transfixed on every word we said.

"We are here in the name of Jesus," we explained.

They responded, "We know! We know!"

"There's a festival coming up and we are offering personal prayer for anyone in the area that wants it." They looked at us and each other with anticipation, so I continued. "The festival is big, and we are not able to pray with everyone during that time, so we come to the villages for prayer."

"We have not been to the festival because we are Muslim," they provided.

Doyle took the lead in the conversation at that point. To be honest, I had no idea what he was saying because I checked out of the moment and into the spirit to see where I was on my spiritual meter. After assessing myself, I felt good that regardless of Doyle's position on the spiritual meter I was back in line. The atmosphere was still very charged with contempt and anger, but I was back in spiritual position with my Heavenly Father's peace.

Doyle and I sat and talked for a few moments bouncing our casual conversations about the children, their home, their country, back and forth when suddenly, I could feel a shift. It was as if the clouds parted, and we were in the eye of the storm.

I seized that moment to ask the question. It was totally out of context. It was not part of where we were in our dialogue. It was just a moment that came upon me that needed to be blurted out during this lull in the storm we felt. "Do you want to know more about Jesus?" The words flew out of my mouth and my translator mimicked the tone with just as much urgency.

She said, "Yes."

I felt like this conversation needed to be expedited...now. I couldn't understand why, but I talked as quickly as my translator could translate. The woman was leaning in, loving the stories of this magnificent Jesus and began to ask questions when I felt the other side of the storm come upon us.

A man came around the corner in his Muslim attire. He was an average size man, but he was large in their eyes, and he was in charge. He didn't stop when he saw us. As a matter of fact, he knew we were there. He never turned to look at me as he passed by. There was silence in his approach and there was silence in all of us as he made his way through us.

There were four of us and several others had gathered to listen while we were there. However, it was as if none mattered. He strode straight through the center of our gathering, past each of us, and directly into the house. The aggression was back in the air. It was now very intense.

The woman I spoke with obediently scurried into the hut after the man, while another woman bolted past us and into the same house without a word.

There was one woman left and there was fear in her eyes. I couldn't help but wonder, "What was going on behind that closed door?" As scared as she was, her curiosity was just as prominent. There was much weight in the air. Doyle got my attention as he indicated we were being watched. Through the window, the only thing visible was the eye of the man and the top of his head. He was crouched down in front of the window, watching, listening, and monitoring.

We were running out of time, and we could all feel it. "Do you wish Jesus to be part of your life?"

As if she was trying to make her decision as quietly as possible, she whispered with eyes darting to and from the door, "Yes." This woman who was in this oppressive and probably abusive atmosphere was willing to take this risk while the danger was literally so close to her.

As we began to pray together, it was as if sandpaper was being rubbed on a raw wound of everyone who began to gather. Irritation, anger, and agitation were all around us. As we prayed to Jesus, more and more people gathered from places unknown less than a foot or two from us. We were surrounded and they were angry.

There was no fear in myself or Doyle. I saw my interpreter looking around, almost nervously, but continued to translate without missing a beat. She repeated every word while holding my hands, and her eyes darted from one person to the next as they multiplied around us. However, the moment the word "Amen" was said, everyone present, scattered.

We looked around us in every direction assessing any threats in the area. Doyle continued to speak while he scanned the area around us. He conveyed to me in English what we were both thinking, "I think she needs protection."

She began walking away. The atmosphere was thick and heavy. The people watched closely. The man continued watching us through the window from his squatted position and everything was silent.

"I agree." With that agreement, I stopped her and prayed protection over her.

While that was intense, it was nothing compared to the woman who was sitting inside of a family "store" surrounded by a metal cage on the outside. There was no light inside this hut with a cage, only a few food items that perhaps would feed two or three people.

I was getting tired from battling such darkness, so I reached out to take my partners hand to see if we could get back into unity. Instead of taking my hand, he placed it on my back and nudged me toward the woman in the cage. Doyle conveyed, "This woman is yours to talk to."

I began talking to her about why we were there, the festival, and Jesus, as had been our normal conversation starter, but there was something else going on that I just couldn't see. She looked at me, held my gaze, then put her head down into her hand and sat quietly.

"I'm Muslim," she said very softly as she looked back over her shoulder.

It was then that I saw she was not alone. There was a man in the shadows of this hut. He was looming and lingering without apology. I could see her struggle and feel the hopelessness in her. She looked at the person hovering just over her shoulder a number of times. He listened to every word and was not happy about it.

The tension continued to rise so I felt that for her safety I would give her a way out of the dialogue. "It's ok. If you ever decide to invite Jesus into your heart and into your life, you can do that silently in your heart and mind." I asked her to consider whether or not she believed that Jesus lived, died, and rose again. I explained that she would just need to ask for forgiveness for her sins, ask Jesus into her heart and her life and allow God to reveal Himself in it. Giving her a quick example of what a prayer to Jesus sounded like, I rattled off a quick prayer and blessing.

"No one can take away your desire to have Jesus in your heart and no one can take away your private conversations with the Lord. That is between you and Jesus."

She knew I was referring to the hovering shadow. Her head was still down during the conversation but when I made that last statement, she raised her eyes so I could see her ever so subtly. She smiled with her head down, her eyes up, and we connected in that moment.

The oppression in this area just kept increasing as we walked. It was thick and still seemed to be working on Doyle. There was a spiritual divide between Doyle and me and there was nothing I could do about it.

Walking up the road a bit further, we noticed two women who had their sewing machines on the front porch of their concrete home making scarves. They barely looked up as we approached and their scowls continued to confirm what I felt, but we smiled and continued to approach. "Hello, we are in town for a festival," handing them the flyers from the festival. Heads down, we heard, "We're Muslim."

Smiling, I intercepted whatever Doyle was getting ready to say, "I know and that's ok. I love you no matter what you choose." It was then that they lifted their heads and smiled. There were children all around us. Some were playing and others sat quietly at our feet staring up at us with interest.

Noticeably, there wasn't a childlike softness in their eyes. Instead, there was anger and emptiness. This place felt empty, lifeless, and full of hatred. Scanning the people there, one was different than all the others. Her eyes were filled with light. Immediately turning my attention to her, I approached as she sat off to the side getting her hair combed by another woman.

More children began to gather. In response to the multiplication of children, the sound level increased and suddenly there were children hiding within the folds of my skirt as if it was a blanket of comfort. I looked down at those children and their eyes were almost glowing in comparison to the previous children that were there just a moment ago. Audibly gasping, I knew which children were hers.

Pointing at several specific children that had the same light in their eyes, I said, "These children have the same special light in their eyes that you do."

The angry woman who was doing the combing immediately put her head in the palm of her hand and looked away but didn't say a word. Her resentment was boiling over, and she could barely contain it. The woman with the light in her eyes just sat silently, holding my gaze, and not moving.

Reflection & Revelation: Looking back at my journal as I wrote this book with more detail, I realized just how often my eyes locked with others and they did not move.

One of these children with the light in his eyes came over to me with his little hand out. He couldn't have been more than three years old. He grabbed ahold of my skirt and just filled his little hand with all the material he could gather. He looked up at me with such sweet big eyes. He continued to hold on while looking around as if he knew me and knew I was safe and ok.

"Are any of these children yours?" I asked the woman with the light.

She responded by pointing at the same children that I had pointed to.

It was breathtaking to witness the tangible difference of the woman with the light having the children with the light, in contrast to the woman with the death in her eyes and the children with death in their eyes. To be honest, to see it in such purity shook me just a bit. I knew the anger around us was heavy and it seemed like a ridiculous question with such a clear rebuke around us, but I had to ask.

"Can we pray with you?"

She looked directly at me as she said, "Yes, please."

We gathered around the woman with light and began to pray blessings and protection over her. She closed her eyes and sat listening intently to the prayer.

Yes, she was Muslim. Yes, those children were Muslim, but their hearts knew something else. She was Muslim by cultural assignment only, because she knew Jesus in her heart.

I was personally affected as we prayed. Not because of the prayer but because it was as if the Lord Himself came down and put His hand right over us.

Tears reflecting the sun at the corners of her closed eyes were evident as she listened to every word the interpreter spoke out. With every statement, every blessing, she nodded in agreement. Her heart was soft.

"Do you want to let go of the Muslim faith?"

She said, "No."

"Do you want to welcome Jesus?"

As she nodded, she did with tears falling from the corners of her eyes. I thought to myself, "This is very interesting," and asked the Lord to show me whatever it was that I needed to know. It was then that I saw the shield. She was walking in the darkness with the shield of light around her. She smiled as I suddenly understood. She was different on the inside than she must live on the outside. Nodding at each other in acknowledgement, we bid her goodbye and continued our journey down the pathway.

The further we walked, the oppression deepened. It got downright creepy feeling. There was a young girl outside of a house. "Is there a big person here?" Without a word, she ran off and toward a doorway to a hut.

We waited a few moments, standing there talking amongst ourselves, I looked up and noticed that we were being watched. There, a few feet from us was a face peeking around the wooden fence that was attached to the hut. I waved to whoever it was to make the statement, "I see you." Quickly, they attempted to disappear from my view. A few moments later, a woman came to another door and looked out at us. To be honest, she looked extremely bad. She was probably in her 30's, but she looked so much older and sad.

She began, "I know who you are. I know Jesus."

Ok, since she knew Jesus, it only made sense that we begin to talk a bit more.

We broke our own rules and asked if we could come in.

She thought for a long moment and said, "Yes."

"I've known Jesus for a long time," she said, but something was off. The house felt heavy. A potent smell of solder and welding material was coming from somewhere. Homes typically have no electricity, and this house was no different, but it wasn't just dark in appearance, it felt dark.

Doyle took the lead, "You said you know Jesus. How do you know him?"

She repeated herself, "I know Jesus."

Something was not adding up. I could feel it. Her face was strained. Doyle rarely confronts someone like this but without warning he said, "There is something wrong with this house."

She looked at him and did not respond. She was actually considering what he just said.

The Holy Spirit ignited in me, "What's going on with your health, mama?"

She sighed, "I have been in the hospital many times this year. They could not find anything, so I know it's spiritual." She went on to say, "I've been going to a prophet or a healer is known everywhere. He invites me every time he's here," as she held a bracelet up that proudly displayed the prophet's name on it.

Running to humans, looking for answers through people who claim to have connection with God seems to be an international hysteria rather than a singular culture.

"There is only One that can heal you and give you answers. His name is Jesus. A true prophet will direct you back to God, never back to themselves." Now, I had her attention, "A true prophet will give you warnings or help to get you back on track through the words God provides, but a true prophet will never create an atmosphere to keep people coming back to them."

She smiled as if a light suddenly came on inside her. She thanked us and we began to make our way to the doorway of the hut, "Do not be fooled by people who direct you to return to them. A prophet of God speaks of God, for God, and about God, but always exalts God above themselves and never asks for money to do it." She cocked her head. I continued, "In the Bible there is none who got paid for telling the truth. The only one who got paid was a traitor, Judas. Save your money and use it for the medicine you need, and the prayer is free." With that, we walked out the door and directly to three men that were standing there waiting. Doyle and his interpreter walked toward another house as the three men watched his departure.

Beginning in Swahili, they stopped me and informed me that they spoke English and knew Jesus. There was a glint of mischief in their eyes. Perhaps it was because I was American, perhaps it was because I was white, or perhaps it was because I was a woman. Regardless, the conversation was going to be different than ALL others.

"You say you know Jesus, so do you speak of Jesus?" Looking at each man individually, I repeated the question and waited for a response.

One by one, they said, "No."

"Do you love Jesus?" I pressed.

"Yes," they each said.

"If you love Jesus, and you know of Jesus, why don't you speak of Him?"

Two men spoke up, "We have no documents."

My mind searched for what they were referring to. Ordinations, legal rights, and cultural approval…then it hit me. They were asking for the Bible.

"Do you mean the Bible?"

One of the men shook his head and lowered his voice, "We cannot get Bible's here, so there is nothing to talk to the people about."

Understanding the concern and potential danger they might be in, I asked, "Do you talk to God every day?"

They looked at me and then each other. They seemed embarrassed at the question. Each one softly admitted, "No."

"If you don't talk to Him and you don't talk about Him, then what kind of relationship do you have WITH Him?" They had no answer. They realized that they knew OF Jesus but didn't truly know Him. "Come to the festival and learn about Jesus' life, His death, and who He is."

Shaking their heads, they each said they were too far from any churches and even farther from the festival.

It was then that I remembered that we did have a Bible in my partner's backpack. "I'll be right back," I assured the men as I strode off in the last direction I saw Doyle walking.

It was so interesting to think, even in that time, in those moments, there was such a boldness in walking out my assignments maneuvering the streets of Africa without contact with anyone except my interpreter. It was so peaceful in my spirit.

"Doyle! Doyle!" as I looked from hut to hut. Locating him in an area ministering to others, I quietly walked up, slid my hand into his backpack, took a Bible, and returned to the men I had been speaking to before.

Their eyes sparkled with joy as they asked me to assign them a verse that applied to them. This was such a beautiful request. Each wanted their own verse to learn, study, and to grow in. They wanted to know Jesus and they wanted to know themselves.

Turning to my interpreter, I asked him to translate a few words to the men that would stay with them. Once they received the words, they smiled and reached for the Bible quickly to read it for themselves. What a beautiful connection was made. They promised to read to each other and to be held accountable to read to and pray for the others. They agreed with excitement, and as I walked away, they were flipping the pages and beginning their quest to know more.

Doyle and I had come back together on the pathway and headed back toward our pickup point. I noticed something was wrong. Pointing down the path, I took Doyle by the arm and said, "There's something in the pathway that wasn't there before."

At first, we thought it was innocent children playing with what they had to play with. Then I saw it and it was a message. It was not a message of love or kindness. The children of the Muslim house with the sewing machines drew a huge snake in the road right where we would be walking through. Doyle and I estimated it to be about thirty feet long and about a foot and a half in width. The boys who created it were the same boys we saw earlier with resentment in their eyes. There were daggers coming out of their eyes toward us, arms crossed, and faces scrunched up in disgust.

Standing next to the thirty-foot snake, we looked around. We were being watched openly and by those who were still hiding. There were many.

Unsure of the message, but sure it was one, a response was needed. Quickly, I asked the Holy Spirit for the response. Looking at Doyle, I said, "Drag your heel across the neck of the snake."

He looked at me "Really?"

"Yes, cut the head off the snake."

With that final action, we turned and visually surveyed those standing around us and those we knew were hiding. Our position was made clear, we would not be intimidated.

As we walked away, there was a tangible lift in the oppression, and I could breathe. My face felt lighter, my shoulders felt lighter, but more importantly, my spirit didn't feel like it was so affected. Looking at Doyle, I noticed his face looked different too. One way to test where we were spiritually was to act on it. Reaching out my hand, he looked over, smiled, and took it. He was back. The softness of Doyle was back. The influence that was trying to change who we were was removed. The principalities may have pressed in on us, but we stood strong.

As we walked out of the village, a few women stopped us to talk. I glanced back to speak to Doyle. It was then that I noticed he had stopped at a shack that was selling local wares. A very primitive clay made hut selling whatever food items or handcrafted items they had.

Doyle had noticed that the man in the shack was the same man from another village that had a little too much to drink the day before. Immediately, he was reminded during that conversation the drunken man had requested a Bible and it just so happened that we had one more left. That's how God works. Provision without waste.

We were in a different village, yet this man was right there in front of us. Out of the hundreds of people we encountered, the one man who asked for a Bible when we didn't have any was about to receive the last one we had. The circumstances under which this occurred even perplexed the man. He was elated and astounded that something like that could have occurred.

Doyle simply replied with truth, "God takes care of all the details."

With that act of God, we called our day a success and made our way back to our pickup point to rest before the night's festival.

Infestation

The second evening of the festival was almost upon us as we walked into the deliverance tent. This was my night in the deliverance tent. Our team was there, as well as a few new translators. They greeted us to let us know they spoke "American" and that they desired to help us with our translations. The tent was already full of people lining three of the four walls.

I had to take a moment and get myself into spiritual position because, to be honest, seeing that many people in such desperate need all looking at me for help was a bit overwhelming. I was aware that the rest of my team was there too but, in that moment, it felt almost as if I was alone. Not because of anything our team did or didn't do but because that's what we do as humans. It's kind of like being one of many people in a crowd and yet you feel like everyone is staring at you, when in truth no one even notices you.

Initially, I wanted to look away and not see the pain in the eyes of the people because there were so many, but I knew I was there on assignment.

"Father, help me," was the only thing I could utter before the atmosphere began to get active.

Blind men and women, demon possessed, cancer patients, untreated HIV patients, Down syndrome babies, active TB patients, stroke victims, people who faint from anxiety, depression, you name it, it was present and sitting all around us.

"The festival has not started for tonight yet. Why are they here?" I asked.

My interpreter explained, "These people walked long distances and have already been sitting here for hours just waiting for prayer."

Sitting a mere few feet from all these sick, oppressed, desperate, and possessed were rows and rows of Pastors waiting to hear what the Americans had come to say, but the local Pastors were doing nothing. Desperate people were standing, sitting, and laying down waiting for prayer. However, the Pastors sat with their eyes diverted. They saw the need and they saw the pain, but did nothing.

Only one man, one Pastor out of dozens, got up and came over to pray. One man, while all others looked bothered as people cried out in pain, fear, or pleading, interrupting their experience with the festival.

When the Pastors did muster up a glance at the people who were manifesting so loudly, the only response seen in their eyes was fear. There were witch doctors in their villages, but they were still unqualified, untrained, and full of fear instead of faith. It felt so ugly. It was that same evening that the Pastors, not sure which one, requested that a tarped wall be created so that they would be separated from the people.

Revolted by this, I asked the leadership there, "Why don't the Pastors help and get involved?"

The response was, "They don't get involved in these types of things."

My mind exploded with, "WHAT?!"

I was fuming when the words flew out of my mouth, "Then they need to step down from their pulpits." My interpreter turned and repeated that to the one Pastor assisting us. That Pastor smiled and shook my hand in agreement.

The festival had not even started, and we were already outnumbered. The sheer number of people seemed insurmountable. Looking back, fear wasn't even a thought or option. We knew our authority and it was time to walk in that authority.

The evening began with a boy around the age of nine who was carried into the tent.

"He has tuberculosis," his mother explained. His chest was extended. His legs were weak and unable to hold his weight. His mother continued, "He's in pain when he breathes." We motioned for a chair to be brought in and asked that she set him in it.

We began to pray for his breathing. Initially, he said he could not take a deep breath but instead, what we witnessed him doing was more of a panting to breathe than actual breathing.

We began to pray.

"Try to take a deep breath."

Obediently, he began making the effort and suddenly the panting was gone, and he was able to breathe. Within moments, he was no longer laboring to breathe. He was breathing freely, deeply, and without pain.

When we took our hands off of him and asked him how he felt, he announced that he had no more pain. He breathed and he smiled. We didn't have a second to take in that miracle before an older woman came over to me.

She pointed to her hips, "I cannot walk without pain. Help me."

"How long has this been painful?" I asked.

"Many years," she replied.

It seemed to be just a classic case of arthritis, but it was clearly very painful. She walked slow, calculated, and with a grimace on her face.

Placing a hand on each of her hips, I began to pray while marching in place. After just a few moments, she began mimicking my movements. As prayers got more robust, so did my movements as they became bigger and quicker. She began to mimic those as well. When I took my hands off of her hips, she kept going.

"How does it feel now?" I asked.

"There is no more pain. The pain is gone," She responded.

"Now pray over yourself," I instructed as she continued to march in place with a smile on her face.

"Any pain?"

"No, all my pain is gone. Thank you and praise Jesus." With that she bounced out of sight with more energy than I could ever muster.

There was a tug on my arm as I watched the woman march away. It was a young girl around twelve years old. Her mother had brought her in to see us out of pure desperation.

She had the sweetest face and said she needed prayer because she was flunking school and had never flunked anything before.

"How odd," I thought to myself. "Prayers for grades in the middle of nowhere?" So, I prayed a standard prayer in English for her to think more clearly and asked her how she felt. To me the prayer felt empty, and I was the one praying it! Something was up. There was something in the way.

That's when she said, "I think I have a demon."

I looked at this sweet face and said, "Wait...what?" She had no outward sign of issues other than the schooling issues. She told my interpreter that she was tormented at school and could not stop manifesting there, so she was failing. "Ok, that's more than just asking for help with my grades!" I thought to myself.

I took one look at her and said through my interpreter, "We are going to cast that demon out now if you like."

She looked at me with huge sweet innocent eyes and nodded, "Yes." I began to pray in English, but there was no response. Instead, she just looked at me with wide eyed innocence.

Remember... these sweet people in this remote village have no idea what language I'm using. One language sounds as random as another. I prayed again in English, but no response. I prayed one more time. However, this time I slid naturally into tongues.

Within two or three words of my prayer language, her eyes rolled to the back of her head moving slightly in different directions. She bent over backward so that her head was on the ground. Her feet were still on the ground and her arms were out to her sides. She began growling and speaking against the prayer.

"Yesu, Yesu." The fight within was raging but she blindly began to repeat the name of Jesus with me as her breathing began to calm. The name of Jesus was soothing the child within the body while the demon tried to ravage her. Her body was responding to the war inside her so much so that there was no reason to support her body in such a contorted position because the demon was strong enough to sustain that position for a while. But the moment the demon left, she collapsed into the hands that were waiting for her to fall.

She was unconscious for a few moments before she opened her eyes. She didn't remember where she was or why she was there. She was perplexed. She fearfully began to dart her eyes around the room, not sure where she was and how she got there.

Her mother asked, "How do you feel?"

The child responded, "I feel so good, better than before."

We gave her some time to compose herself as she got up and began to walk away. "The demon is gone. My daughter is back. Thank you."

Hearing that, the child turned and said, "Thank you Miss Pastor," with a huge smile.

In this atmosphere, people are continuously pulling on your clothing, your arms, or tapping on your back to get your attention. Everyone is in triage, and everyone needs help.

A child came to me and with urgency pulled me over to a woman that was about six feet tall.

"What do you need?" I asked.

"I am HIV positive, and I cannot afford the treatments." She held out her arms, "Please pray for my blood to be cleansed."

I was no more finished with that woman when there was a scuffle of sorts going on behind me. Someone was manifesting again, and it wasn't of a smaller scale. It was a dramatic escalation of activity that seriously needed my attention.

Each time the chaos shifted, I found myself shifting, as I'm sure my teammates did as well. Satan and the evil that is doing his bidding watch and learn each of us. As the darkness modifies itself to accommodate what they are observing, it is equally important that we, as soldiers of God, use the discernment to shift in the spirit. It is foolish to stick with formulas. Jesus never used formulas. Jesus knew that the enemy was cunning. So, without question, it's imperative that we continuously check back into the spirit to determine if our responses are flesh driven, habit driven, or spiritually driven.

Looking around, I found myself ministering to one person after another, not really even taking a moment to breathe. I stepped back for just a moment to recheck the spirit to make sure I stayed on track. It was then that something kept hitting against my foot and ankle. Since the tent was so full, I initially didn't pay any specific attention to it. Person after person was brought to me and I just kept ministering with total focus on what was in front of me. The pounding on my foot kept increasing. It was then that something hit me so hard it almost knocked my foot out from under me.

Looking down, there was a woman who was manifesting. Her manifestations were powerful. She was trying to bite everyone and everything that got in her way. I saw the locals poking at her, pushing her, and grabbing her face to try and control her.

"No!" I turned and yelled at each and every one of them as my interpreter worked to keep up. "Unacceptable! This is a human being!"

Turning back around, I wedged myself between her and the other bodies that were manifesting on the ground around us. I physically pushed away all the remaining hands and fingers that were assaulting this woman's body. These people may live in this atmosphere, but they didn't understand how to cast out demons without torment.

I glanced over as someone's hand grabbed at the cheeks of someone that was manifesting on the ground. They grabbed on tightly to her cheeks and shook them back and forth in an effort to "show force over the enemy." Without thought, I put my hand over that person's hand and physically removed the grip from the manifesting person's face.

Looking up at the sea of faces, I ordered them, "Back away!" My interpreter was conveying my orders word for word and with the same emphasis. "Back away right now and leave them alone." I was on my knees in the dirt with a manifesting woman, looking up at dozens, if not more, angry faces all yelling, pointing, and trying to grab at her. Something inside me rose up, and I pushed each one back. Raising my finger, to each one telling them, "No, get back," as they tried to force their way onto this woman. It felt like something out of a movie. My job was to protect the woman and to push back on any conflict while she was so vulnerable. Casting out the demon was secondary in that moment.

Once each aggressive face realized I wasn't backing down, they gave me the respect of walking away. Now it was just her and I. All the sound around us was just background noise as I turned my attention to her spiritual torment now that her physical torment was delt with.

In that setting, it's impossible to know whose hands or arms belong to who. It's just a sea of body parts on the ground, screaming, reaching, or thrashing. This particular young lady seemed to be in her thirties. Her eyes rolled back and then refocused only to say that she hated someone and roll back again. She was growling and speaking in demonic tongues, which was also the norm. She was jerking violently from side to side, whipping her head from left to right, like a caged animal. She gave a sudden jerk, and I felt my shoulder strain a bit, but no pain, so I continued. Manifestations are not seizures but are similar visually.

I took a moment to determine what was occurring. I put this woman onto my lap, I stroked her forehead and pleaded Jesus over her, repeating, "Yesu, Yesu," over and over. Jesus. The more I repeated it, the calmer she got. Softly but firmly, I began to order out the demon that was afflicting her and within moments, she was calm. I rolled her over to her side and a few moments later she began vomiting out the spirit that was holding her captive.

After the conflict in the tent with the locals and the woman was up and safe, I turned to one of the male team members in our group and told him I was stepping out of the tent to assess my shoulder. She was jerking and grabbing with such force I needed to regroup.

As I stepped out, more people were being carried in. Most were manifesting and fighting. I quickly assessed myself, did a spiritual check, and headed back into the tent. As I stepped back in, my attention went to a woman in a grey shirt that was now thrashing around with seven men trying to hold her down to keep her from hurting herself or them. Again, I knew my place, to show authority instead of force.

I laid my hands on her head to determine her spiritual response. She opened her eyes and I saw that she felt the love. I pushed everyone back and put her head on my lap. She knew I was there, but she was unable to speak. She thrashed, flopped, and beat with force, anything that was in her way, but she never took her head off my lap. "Yesu......Yesu......Yesu..." As the name of Jesus was repeated, the calm seeped in. Once the calm settled over her, I was able to cast out the spirit that was holding her hostage.

Over and over throughout the evening, this type of scene reoccurred, until it was a blur of sound and a flurry of activity.

I looked up and noticed that it was getting dark outside. I recall yelling out to someone, "What time is it?"

We were swarmed with people jockeying for our assistance, but we had 15 minutes until the departure time. We had no choice but to begin making our way out. Just at that time, another woman began yelling over the overwhelmingly loud place.

Looking at my interpreter I yelled back, "What is she saying?"

"She says her head and chest are hurting."

I began making my way over to her. The number of people everywhere is almost impossible to describe. Trying not to fall over all those who were manifesting, I approached her without saying a word. Not that she could have heard me if I had spoken anything.

I raised my hand to her forehead and just before making contact, she manifested. Her eyes rolled back into her head. She began to collapse. I caught her, taking all of her weight on my injured arm. Yet again, the Lord held my shoulder in place, and I was without pain.

Time was running out quickly for me to make my way out of there to get to our exit point. Finding a safe position on the ground away from all the feet and the bodies that were thrashing all around us, I placed her unconscious body down. Looking around for assistance and finding none, I quickly cast off the demon leaving her free of pain.

I turned and saw my exit was being blocked by dozens of people, but I was determined to stay in peace. Pushing past all the men who had been standing there keeping several women from running out, I made my way into the open air of the festival and joined our team as we awaited our vehicles.

Warning or Preparation?

For years, I had seen visions of me standing in front of thousands of people preaching the gospel but dismissed it as just a childhood dream. I not only ignored it, but I crushed it as, "What a ridiculous thought." However, in the months preceding the mission trip, the visions began again. "But why?"

That night, after our evening in the prayer/deliverance tent, we gathered back at the bungalows. Out of the blue, the lead Evangelist said that he felt I was supposed to pray the following day. I agreed, thinking that it was just the team he was referring to. It was then that he explained, "Would you be willing to come up on stage and pray for the people over the microphone tomorrow?"

It was as if my vision was playing out in front of me. I was so honored and caught off guard. I know I looked stunned. Without hesitation, I accepted. He had no idea that he was fulfilling a vision that I had seen many months before. I didn't believe it would occur as I was seeing it. Yet it did.

Not having the opportunity to ever hear Ashby on stage prior to the first day and none since, I didn't know the tone of the way he preached. I started to get into my flesh, "What if I pray in a way that insults this culture? What if I don't match the tone of what he's prayed? What if I say something that is conflicting what has already been preached?" My head began to spin with, "What if I mess it up?"

I wanted to honor the Lord and honor the Evangelist. I wanted to speak something that would convey the Lord's will and dovetail into the Pastor's message. The problem was I had no idea what his message was for that day.

Taking deep breath, I needed to get myself into a spiritual place and reject this fleshly worry that had crept in. "First things first, prayer and rest," I thought to myself.

The next morning, I went to God with pen and pad in hand, "What is to be spoken that night?" As I began to receive the answers, I wrote everything down. I was confident that I was prepared because I had the words of God written down in front of me. I was ready! "Nothing would get in my way now!" or so I thought.

That evening, I sat on stage next to Janice. We looked over the audience and listened as the preaching began. As the lead evangelist spoke, I realized that his words and word structure was familiar to my ears. I opened up my pad of paper and followed word for word. Sitting next to Janice, I showed her the pad of paper, and she could hear that he was matching every topic and even the word structure.

The evangelist was speaking the words the Lord gave me line by line. Word for word, I heard what the Lord gave me spoken from the loud speaker. Everything I had obediently written on the page would be spoken by Ashby from the stage that night. I knew what he was going to say next because I was looking at it. Right there on my lap.

I was stunned a bit now, faced with the reality that I had nothing to say when I was called to the microphone. He had already said everything! I reflected on what I had asked of God. "What is going on God?!" I said under my breath as we sat on the stage. It was then that it was made clear, I had asked, "What was to be spoken that night?" I didn't ask what was to be spoken by ME.

Holy Ground

Each night, the lead Evangelist was like clockwork. He had a rhythm and he kept it.

We had come to learn, for those of us who were in the deliverance tent, that once he began to speak the Gospel and call people to Jesus, manifestations would multiply in the crowd. When the call to God was being spoken, the number of manifesting bodies being carried into the tent multiplied faster than we could make room for them. What struck me was the consistency of God's power. God was clearly in control.

However, that night was different. Instead of the lead evangelist conveying the Gospel and calling people to Jesus, the microphone was now handed to me. As I stood in front of thousands of people, I realized God had removed me from any comforts I had written and showed me in a spectacular, inconceivable way that "it's already done." I just needed to let the Holy Spirit flow. The spirit inside me ignited and within a tenth of a second Holy Spirit came rolling out of my mouth.

What He did next was so intensely intimate I could barely restrain myself. As I began to speak the power of God, just as it was laid into my spirit, no holds barred, I looked across the crowd and pointed to the ground in front of my feet declaring, "This ground is now **Holy ground!**"

The words were no more out of my mouth when the atmosphere responded. Fist fights in the crowd broke out as the demons responded to the decree. The darkness within them enraged while the Spirit of the Lord pressed in. It was as if those who were oppressed were now in a trance. Those who were throwing the punches wavered between demonic stares and almost zombie like expressions. Some moved as if they didn't have control over their own bodies as they responded with violence, but their heart wasn't in the battle, something else was.

The fighting initially began in front of the stage right below my feet. Eyes rolling into the back of their heads, they began thrashing violently throughout the crowd. I watched as I spoke. People passed by the stage as they were carried out one after another. They kicked, drooled, growled, bit, and swung their arms wildly. Sounds that were not quite human came from their mouths. Screams that were closely related to the sounds of something animal like. Growling and wide-eyed unfocused stares followed by malevolent mocking laughter were everywhere. These were the sounds of insanity.

From the stage, I continued, "Every **demon must bow to the name of Jesus!**" With that sentence the manifestations in the crowd increased.

I continued, "Every demon must kneel at the feet of Jesus." Again, the manifestations increased.

The Lord was speaking through me. My body was shaking with a trembling that was like a raging river from heaven. This was not adrenaline. This was a power from above that I could not contain. My hand had a grip on the microphone, but my hand was barely able to hold it still.

Apparently, God was not done with me. The next few sentences even confused me. "Do not say no to Jesus, because He said yes to you!" With that sentence, everything inside of me was flooded and I would dare say over-flowing with the Holy Spirit.

The flood, the surge that I was experiencing was barely containable. Those who never experienced the flood of the Holy Spirit would say its adrenaline. I will testify that adrenaline can't hold a candle to the flood of the Holy Spirit. I've experienced both throughout my life, many times. Holy Spirit flood is like a rushing river that creates so much peace, yet an urgency to speak the words that are flooding in. It feels like something I've only experienced within the spirit.

Speaking in public is nothing new to me at this time of my ministry. I've spoken at conferences, on the radio, podcasts, gatherings, teleconferences, videos, and taught classes. Speaking is no longer a fear of mine. But when the Holy Spirit takes over my tongue, the information that comes from my mouth is beyond any human knowledge and far beyond my own understanding or wisdom.

There's a reason that God placed the Holy Spirit inside of us. If we are tapped in, we cannot go wrong. Often, the words and information come so fast it feels as if I'm speaking at an incompressible speed and just trying to keep up. There's a noticeable change in the enunciation and the cadence and the power of projection that comes from the vocal cords. It's not something that's manufactured unless you are a professional speaker, of which I am not.

This particular time, I was lifted up in a way that will never be definable as long as I'm on this earth. It was peace. It was power. It was an urgent focus on hard truths. It was an authority that I don't know how to describe. It was amazing! It may have been my body on that platform, but it was not me that was up there. Holy Spirit did the work. The spirit was overwhelming me, and I yielded. God issues us the assignments, but will never give an assignment without the anointing, power, and coverage to back it up. God's coverage and provision is endless. From the names on the page to the music that followed, it was all anointed.

After I finished, I turned and took my seat. The scheduled singer and her dancers began to perform. Lo and behold, as the lyrics were translated to me, they came to life. She was declaring the ground we walk on to be **"Holy ground"** and that demons must **"bow at the name of Jesus."**

My head began to spin…"What?! Are you kidding?" My mind could not grasp that the words that the Lord gave me were part of their predetermined song line up. I had no idea who these people were, never heard their music, and to this day, have no idea what the name of their group is. But God lined it all up…This was the ultimate lineup. The words on the page spoken by a man who never saw them. The words I spoke flowed out like a river and the people who practiced and prepared their song choices reflected what was conveyed! And none of us spoke to one another! Praise God!!!

I watched the pre-choreographed detail spoken exclusively in Swahili and was in tears. God is clearly in control.

The Next Level

The next evening at the festival, a woman was brought into the deliverance tent in full manifestation. She was intentionally as loud as she could possibly be over all the noise and chaos. Her level of aggression was intense. Her goal was to interrupt the momentum of people listening and accepting Jesus as their Lord and savior. She flailed her arms and kicked anyone, with the intention to inflict pain with every blow. Her movements were indiscriminate in who they hurt. Her goal…Pain, distraction, and attention.

Several people, mostly men, began to restrain her. It took a minimum of five people at any given time. She was well dressed, wearing a white lace dress. She quickly earned the name Legion from me as I watched her writhing on the ground cursing wildly. Her eyes went from squinting to wild-eyed to a mocking glare. She was fighting everyone with all her might while laughing in what could only be defined as a loathsome, spite-filled, mocking cackle.

The enemy inside her was contorting her body to make it more difficult to keep her held in place and attempting to bite when possible. As she laughed and snarled, she began asking for "the white man," growling through clenched teeth.

I looked in her eyes, and my protective instincts began to flare. "You're not messing with Doyle," was my immediate thought. There were three white men on this team. Two on stage and one here in the tent. I wasn't sure which one she was looking to get ahold of, but Doyle was the closest in proximity to her, so Doyle was my immediate concern. Through squinted stare, my thoughts were not very minister like as I responded with, "That would be a very bad choice for her to act on. That's one spiritual battle I would not shy away from."

There is a weird space that I know all too well about me. It's not a place of flesh and it's not totally in the spirit. It's somewhere in between. It's a boundary. It's rather hard to explain. When I am in that spirit-filled space, there is an abundance of love and compassion. However, when that boundary line is crossed, a feeling of supercharged supernatural "energy" shows up inside me. It's something that has been consistently present in my life since I was a small child. It will back up the biggest demon and knock them on their butt. It's not something I can plan for or ask for; it just shows up as God deems it necessary.

Her maniacal laugh continued as she asked over and over for the "white man." Doyle was within sight and sound of this woman. Without thinking, I looked at him and motioned for him to stay back.

There was chaos all around this woman. One of the interpreters turned to me and said, "She's calling out to other demons asking for more power." That was all I needed to hear. It confirmed that we were dealing with something akin to Legion.

Every time she became weakened by our using the name of Jesus, she would call out for additional demons to infuse her with more. One of the interpreters asked me in my ear, "Why can't you just cast it out?"

I didn't realize at that moment I was about to speak prophetically, but I did…"Because she's in covenant with them." In the coming months, I learned of the depth of that prophetic word and the choices that she made regarding the Legion.

Legion changed her demands from the white man to demanding the "Pastor" in the same in a mocking tone. Turning to the interpreter I asked, "What is she referring to?"

"She wants the evangelist on stage."

Legion was on a power trip and her requests were denied.

One of the Pastors on our team, Kaden, was one of those who was actively holding down Legion. He was amazing in his restraint as he sang over the woman, hosing Legion and taking authority to calm the manifestations as needed.

Bouncing back and forth between the immediate needs and Legion, I watched Kaden as he continued to sooth and protect the woman. In between the incoming demands, I would turn my attention back to Legion. Kneeling next to her crazed body, I also spoke Jesus over her and rebuked the curses that she spoke out against each member of our team.

I don't know how Kaden was able to maintain physical or mental strength during such a long-term battle. It was a full-on clash of dark and light. Our saving grace was that each of us, with the exception of Jezebel, were strong and seasoned in spiritual battles. Had any one of us fallen into any flesh-based reactions, the entire scene would have gotten completely out of control. To be honest, if we had allowed ourselves to slip into the flesh and respond in violence, we would have had the manpower to destroy or kill the woman who was actively trying to hurt us.

The dark spirits were pushing us to what they perceived as "the brink," but we had plenty of God and Holy Spirit in our personal reserves. The chaos was around us, but we were peaceful. Tired...but peaceful.

We were being baited by the underworld. The underworld, the dark, and evil entities do not care about the woman, the host. They would not care if we were to respond to the woman from a position of personal offense or defense. It was up to US to use our discernment, rather than responding to what we saw. It's only through discernment that we could understand that we were not battling with the woman. We were not interested in hurting the woman as a defensive action. We were there to protect others while restraining the actions of the demonic. We were there to be like Jesus and nothing less. As maturity in Christ continues to grow, the heart of Jesus takes over and redirects our paths. That includes our choices, reactions, and responses.

The rest of the evening was like the previous. People were being carried in faster than we could get to them. The sounds were unearthly, the combat was consistent, and the needs just kept growing.

One evening, for some reason, Jezebel joined us in the tent. My immediate thought was "bad decision." Looking at Jezebel in the tent, I asked, "You sure you want to do this?"

Her pride was still running unchecked as her cocky response came from her lips, "I've seen many manifestations."

My thoughts immediately went to the previous few days, "So she lies, sets me up, invokes the leadership as her scapegoat, tried to tear me down, tore apart the scriptures, and now she's amongst the demons. Who in the world thought this was safe for anyone?!" That was as far as my thoughts had time to go because

I was too busy with what was going on around me to go any further in discussion about her being there.

She, being so willing to partner with the dark spirits, was a beacon for the demonic and it showed. About a half hour into all the chaos, I had looked over to check on my team members. Each of us were on our knees, leaning over helping, praying, or dealing with ministry requests. Then I saw Jezebel.

Jezebel was overwhelmed, standing in one spot, looking in shock, not talking to anyone, and doing nothing. "Someone needs to get her out of here," I thought to myself. "She's an open door." All the while, people were crying out in pain, manifesting, and asking for help all around her. She looked right passed them, doing nothing.

I made my way over to her and asked her if she was ok. She looked at me with the same smirk, "I'm fine."

She had absolutely no business being there. Once she was there, she realized the same thing, but what she didn't realize (or maybe she did) was the side we were battling was the same side that she was on. Where was her self-proclaimed strength now? This was no place for pride. For her own spiritual safety, she needed to be dismissed from the tent, but I was a little bit busy with all that was going on and she wouldn't have listened anyway. Pride was present.

"If you're on prayer support, maybe you should pray outside the tent because this is getting rough in here," I suggested. I didn't have time to listen to her response as in that moment I noticed someone pulling at my arm from another direction. A woman was manifesting, kicking, and screaming, while her eyes rolled back. I went over and put the woman's head on my lap, again stopping people from restraining her.

She was so haunted by what she was seeing in the spirit, she looked deeply traumatized already with her current state, and strangers holding her down was only serving to feed the trauma. Getting the people off of her, I looked into her eyes and spoke the name of Jesus. I watched as the demon retreated. Her body responded. The kicking and writhing stopped and now she laid peacefully in my lap, her eyes distant and empty, and her breathing labored.

A classic move of the demonic is for the evil spirit to hide when they are confronted with something that might remove them from their host. I gave her a moment to rest rather than calling the demon forward. I took authority over where it retreated to and revoked its residency. Within seconds, I saw her eyes clear and turned her over to vomit out the darkness. I waited for her to finish vomiting, then watched as she became aware of her surroundings.

"You're safe. The demon is gone," I explained.

She didn't know how she got there or what occurred. Her memory of the entire event was gone. She shook her head, still in shock, and took my hand. "Thank you," she said with her eyes still full of confusion as she tried to take in the scene. Smiling, I told her she was loved.

Meanwhile, in the background, Legion was still screaming, fighting, biting, and kicking, but before I could turn my attention back to the ruckus of Legion, there was another young lady clearly manifesting. She was not manifesting in the traditional sense. She was quiet, smirking, evil in her eyes, not writhing or seeking attention. This one was devious. "Do you speak English?" I shocked myself. "Why would I ask her that? I've not asked anyone else if they spoke English," I thought.

She did not respond. She just stood there, staring with the same devious and challenging look on her face. The interpreter asked her the same thing and then turned to me saying, "No, she does not." He explained that she's a simple uneducated woman and a bit crazy.

"Why are you here?" I asked. I was direct and to the point.

"I have a pain." She pointed to her stomach and then again to her head.

Looking at her, I could see why. She was only half present. This demon was not hiding inside, it was standing right in front of me. There was very little of the woman left, but there was enough of her left to ask for help.

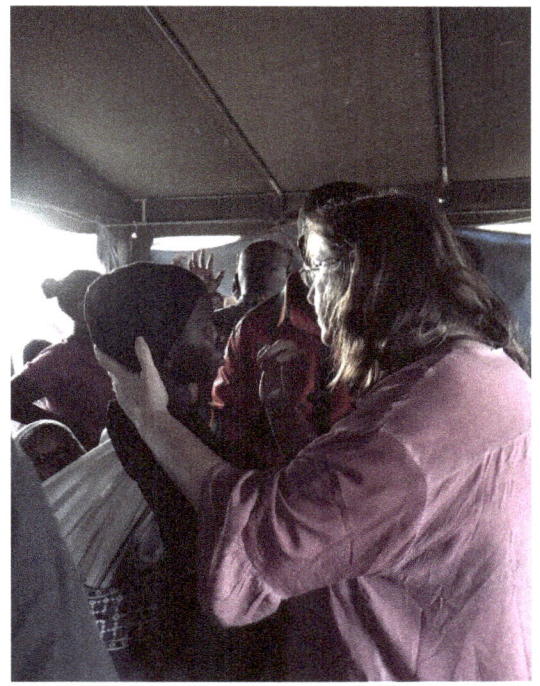

I placed my hand on her head and began praying in my spirit language. She fully manifested. I continued in my prayer language but at some point, I flipped back to English and she began responding to my English commands accurately. "Wait a minute. She doesn't speak English, but she's responding to English accurately," I thought to myself.

It suddenly occurred to me what was happening. The demons were responding in English, while the woman remained incapacitated within her own body. I made a mental note and went back to the task of casting out the little maniacal, English speaking demon and waited for her to regain herself. Once she was back to a solid place of awareness, I asked her a few questions in English. She couldn't understand a word.

By this time, Legion was out of hand. I got back down on my knees slightly behind her right shoulder. Legion was sitting in an upright position with people all around restraining her. Kaden prayed and called out the demon that was manifesting, ordering the demon out of the body of this woman. At this point, he had things well in hand, so all I did was put my hands on her shoulder and back to pray. As soon as my hands made contact, her head turned, and she spit with complete accuracy into my face.

My only thought was not to allow the attempt at provocation to get any response in the spirit, to remain at peace while this battle waged. In the flesh, I might have been tempted to punch her in the face, but that is not where my spirit was. My spirit was full of sadness for her choices and compassion for her position. It wasn't her that spat in my face, it was the demon.

I grabbed her face and jaw on my side, as others did the same, but she was incredibly strong. With little to no effort and without any real pause, she turned her head again. The second time she spit was just as accurate as the first. She again bypassed all others and responded directly to my presence. I had no idea if she did this to others, but I got the feeling that she had not by Kaden's response. I wasn't the one holding her down, yet the demons were responding with anger and offense to me.

She turned her head and loaded up to spit for a third time. This time Kaden took his hand towel and covered Legion's mouth to prevent her from spitting again. This didn't seem to deter her determination. Her mouth remained covered as she did her best to bite and spit more.

I will never forget his actions in stepping in with his pastor's towel, but there was no time for thank you. Legion continued to whip and jerk toward me, trying to close the gap between us. Kaden and I gripped her by her shoulders to hold her in place. Again, the hysterical laughter came from her with a look in her eyes that was not of this earth. It was lunacy in her eyes. With a sudden strength that seemed to come from nowhere, she began to force herself up off the ground, pushing against all those who had restrained her. She had more strength than a man.

She began chanting, "I do not fear Jesus." She continued alternating from challenging the power of Jesus to "give me the white man" and never seemed to run out of energy.

Again, my skirt got pulled and I left Legion and Kaden long enough to handle the rest of the needs. I looked back at Kaden. He was dripping with sweat on his forehead. He had so much stamina it had to be God's strength because it was a relentless battle.

The hours flew by, and night was upon us. We exited the tent to gather and find our rides. Without a word, I grabbed a bottle of water that I found and Doyle's handkerchief out of his hand. Wetting the handkerchief, I wiped my face over and over to get the demon spit off. Once I got back to my room, the next thing to go was my clothing. A dress I loved had to be discarded because there was no way I was bringing that dress back home to my grandchildren. While any real risk was almost nonexistent, it was worth leaving behind that DNA.

The Final Battle

During the day, Doyle and I did our walk in the villages. By now, we had walked many miles every day and followed it with nightly battles. He and I were both exhausted and wondered if we had any more fuel inside us to get through the next few days, but we were there to do a job, so we prayed up, guzzled down some water, and prepared for "the tent."

That night in the tent there was a man, as well as many others who waited two to three rows deep. As we walked in, all the attention immediately swung to our presence. I could see the anticipation in everyone's eyes. We were dog tired, but we focused. I looked at the first man I noticed when we came in. He was a pastor that had suffered a stroke. He could not speak, could not lift his arms, or walk without assistance. Doyle had great success the day before with praying for healing. I called, "Doyle can you come here? I need you."

Doyle made his way over to me and the man and asked what was needed.

"He had a stroke."

Without any further explanation Doyle and I began to pray. He in English and me in my prayer language. I took my position kneeling in front of him praying for his hands and feet while Doyle prayed for his arms and hands. When the prayer seemed to just shut off, I stood.

"Sir, please lift your arms," I requested.

The man didn't understand, so my partner again asked him to lift his arms and demonstrated.

We had an interpreter, but it was too loud in the tent. After seeing Doyle's demonstration, he lifted his arms.

"Yes! Can you lift them higher?" we asked.

He did. That's when he said, "Halleluiah!" Doyle and I just looked at each other. He just spoke!!

We went back into prayer, me in tongues and my partner English. Without a word, the man got up and started walking and kept walking. He was so excited that he could walk, he continued right out of the tent with his arms moving normally. He walked so far, we had to stop him and have him return to his wife back in the tent. Needless to say, he could now walk.

Again, there was someone pulling on me from behind. This time it was a woman. Doyle was saying goodbye to the "walking man" and I was focused on the sight of his smile as I turned around. Immediately, there was a woman directly in my face. She was staring at me. Without a word, she placed a baby in my arms. As soon as the baby was in my arms, she began to speak. Quickly, I called out to my interpreter over the sound of the roaring tent.

"What is she saying?"

He turned and asked for her to repeat what she said.

"Help me and my baby."

"What is wrong?" I asked.

"The baby does not move. The baby does not kick his legs."

I had this little child in my arms, and I was being knocked around by all the people manifesting. My maternal instincts took over. I knew I needed to get this child to a safer place.

She went on to explain, "The baby's hands are so weak they cannot hold anything." After listening to the desperate plea of this pained mother, I looked around for a place of safety. Finding a wall of the tent I could tuck in against, I knelt down and placed the baby crossways on my lap. Once settled safely against the tent wall, I was able to finally look down at the baby's sweet face. I immediately saw the problem. Down syndrome. I asked the mother, "Has anyone said the words Down syndrome when the baby went to the doctor?"

She said, "No, only that the baby's brain didn't work right."

Again, I reached forward and pulled on my partners arm to get his attention. He turned toward me, and I pointed to the baby. Like the true man of God that he is, I saw his heart melt and he laid hands on the baby with me. Holding the baby in my arms, I began to pray. I began to press forward on the baby's legs so that they were bending at the knee and the baby began to kick against me. I Repeated this several times and again the baby kicked.

"Mama, how long has he been able to kick?" I asked.

"That was the first time that my baby has kicked," she replied.

"How old is this baby?" I asked the question remembering that most have no idea when they were born. I was surprised when the mother responded, "My baby is eleven months old."

Shocked at this little frame I was holding, I pointed to the baby, "This baby is eleven months old?"

She confirmed that indeed that baby was just short of one year old.

"Wow," my brain could not compute that. At most, I would have thought he was three to four months old.

I began to pray over his little hands. As I did, I put my pinky finger in the baby's hand. Nothing. I continued to pray and did it again and again nothing. A third time I repeated this, and I watched as the baby grabbed onto my pinky. I switched to my thumb. The baby grabbed onto my thumb. "Mama, how long has he been doing that?" I asked.

Her eyes were shining with excitement, "Never! He's never held anything or grabbed anything. He just lays there."

Again, I put my thumb back in the baby's grip and pulled upward. The baby resisted and pulled down on my thumb. "You must ask the Lord for more for your baby and give all glory to God. Every day do what I did until he is moving better." I handed the baby back to his mother and got up off the ground.

I wasn't even in a full standing position when I turned around and another woman was standing there with a baby slung over her back. "I have a demon. I need help." She described pain in her head and her womb. Knowing that so many of these manifestations result in contortions, I was concerned about the baby on her back. Taking the baby off of her wasn't an option with the combative surroundings. Somehow, God was going to make this work, so my job was just to trust in that. I placed my hands on her shoulders. Initially, I restricted my prayer to English, but when I saw no change, I allowed myself to go into the Spirit. It was that moment that my concern became a reality. She began to manifest. To protect the baby, I ordered the demon to not manifest. Immediately, the demon receded and evaporated. Placing my hand on her stomach and head, I spoke the name above all names, "Jesus take over her body."

Hearing a familiar chaos, I followed the sound to the opening of the tent. Again, Legion was being carried into the tent. Again, she manifested in the crowd and began assaulting people.

P. Frederick

These were the last two days of the festival. We were all tired but as the people began to be carried in, the Holy Spirit fired up and we were full of energy.

Supercharged

I made a mental note that Legion was placed into a chair and surrounded by people who kept her restrained. As the evening wore on, I walked past the chair in the confined space of the tent. It was at that moment when Legion broke free of the six people and lunged her hand toward me.

This time she was able to make contact. She reached for my throat with accuracy and speed. Suddenly, everything seemed to be moving slow and controlled in my mind. I too had pinpoint accuracy playing out in real time. I remember her eyes. We locked eyes and with complete accuracy my hand was able to grab her wrist while unconsciously going into a spiritual language that I've never used before.

I know my spiritual language. I have several, but this one was filled with an intensity that I have not yet experienced. It was power packed.

As soon as my hand came in contact with hers, she weakened from this powerful entity that just got away from six people to setting her back down myself. Again, she was restrained.

As chaos continued to amplify all around us, I looked around mindlessly taking note of the area in which I was standing. Again, people were being carried in at such a rate it appeared as if the tent walls should just be removed and fill the area. My mind was almost numb with exhaustion and being outnumbered.

Bodies of people laying in every direction, screaming into nothingness, crying out for Peace. Wailing for help because there is a demon tormenting them. Empty stares that seem to be filled with horror that see nothing but whatever they are seeing in their heads or in the spirit. People with eyes rolling in two different directions and bodies that arch backwards onto their own heads while their feet are still on the ground in front of them. Then there are those people who are fighting a spirit that is standing in front of them that only they can see but their response is to fight, kick, and bite.

Looking around with the same numb mind, I observed that there was no place left for us to physically stand, no place to kneel to minister to the people. It's truly a war. It was something not of this world.

Reengaging my brain, I moved to lean over a very sick woman. I was totally focused, hearing what the woman had to say when out of nowhere, Legion came up out of her chair and made her final move.

It was as if I felt her coming and spun around just in time to hear her begin to utter another demonic curse in my direction. Without any thought whatsoever, I quickly spoke in that new power-filled tongue. The intensity was heard over whatever she was saying. My hand came up in front of me in a strange position. I watched my body respond while feeling a surge of liquid authority rolling through it. The curse she was speaking was in Swahili. However, somehow, I knew what she was speaking. Interesting. As I write this, I just received revelation. I understood her Swahili curse, but I couldn't understand her demonic tongue... "Interesting... So now I understand Swahili?"

My hand was up in front of me, and I didn't know why. It was in a half "c" position with my fingers spread facing her. The power tongue flew out of my mouth with no thought. The wave of liquid authority surging and coursing through from above, down through my chest, igniting my inner man even more so that it felt like sparks were flying inside of me.

I watched her eyes widen with fear. Her mind was locked with her own inner knowing of what was occurring. I was in a tongue that should not be understood, but it was a language that was directed to the Father of the Universe. It was His power that was now moving through me. Heaven and earth were meeting. Right then. Right there and she knew it. Her words kept coming as if she was on auto pilot. There was no power. Her intensity was gone, and she was slowly weakening in front of my own eyes. I began to lean my upper body into the direction of my hand. I was literally driving the Holy Spirit into her direction. There was a distance of at least three feet between us, but she rapidly backed up as if I was almost on top of her. There was no hiding the fact that she was visibly shaken by what the Holy Spirit was declaring.

As she backed up, her words began to fumble from her lips, but she never looked away. My words remained clear and strong as hers tapered off into just empty movements of her mouth. It was as if the demons kept pressing forward on their performance until they no longer could.

She finally backed up enough to run into the chair behind her and fell into the seat. Almost simultaneously, I noticed the five to six people who had been previously restraining her watching me intensely. Not moving, not reaching, and not changing their position by the chair. Some of them with their mouths open in confusion. Once she fell back into the chair, they moved in to restrain her once again. I looked around the people who restrained her, and Kaden was not among them.

I should have known that if Kaden wasn't there speaking Jesus over her, Legion would regroup and try again. Lesson learned, make sure whoever has your back is strong enough in the spirit to truly have your back. In other words, anyone who does not truly know their authority in the spirit and has never tested it, has no business standing in a position of authority. I don't know where Kaden was during this time and perhaps he joined the scrum of Legion after that moment, I just didn't know.

Turning back around, I resumed ministering to the people as we had in days prior. Again, people were coming in and the needs were growing. Time marched forward into the day and as I stood bent over ministering to a man who had an illness, I felt something hit me from behind.

Without warning, Legion had gotten loose and grabbed me from behind. She jumped fully onto my back and wrapped her arms around my shoulders. Her feet were off the ground and now I was holding her full weight as she grappled for my throat as I was bent over this man in prayer. My stance and footing were not prepared for this extra weight, yet my body did not waver.

My friend Danielle looked over and witnessed Legion on top of my back. Legion was screaming and cackling in my ear. Her hand was still trying to get to my throat. Yet without any thought, an amazing peace came over me. Everything was again in a slow controlled motion in my mind. I was hyperaware of everything and yet nothing at the same time.

From that point, it was no longer me responding, but something powerful inside of me. Without any assistance from anyone, I single-handedly stood up with her on my back. I took

Legion's hands from my neck and throat, removed both of her arms from my body, and threw her off of me without any effort.

Now remember, my shoulder was in bad condition. Dislocating at random, debris in my shoulder in places it shouldn't have been, torn rotator cuff, torn labrum, and damage to my humerus, bicep tendon, as well as clavicle. However, that is not an issue when we are moved supernaturally. The sheer magnitude of the strength I felt surging through me in that moment was unearthly.

After she was thrown off me, I spun around for the next attack. My interpreter saw Legion charging at me one more time. However, this time he was in position to intervene by slapping Legion across the face. This stunned her long enough for people to grab her once more and return her to her chair without any resistance.

This was our last night there and she gave it her best effort, but God's coverage is unmatched. As we cleared the tent, seeing that all who had come for help had been indeed ministered to, we began to praise Jesus for what He accomplished that night.

We stood in the center of the tent taking in the events of the last several days. A woman who had been with us for the previous few days approached. Without a word, she got on her knees and wrapped herself around the legs of Kaden. She then stood, walked over to me, and knelt in front of me wrapping herself around my feet and legs. She then rose to bow in honor. Next, she moved on to Doyle and repeated the same honoring action.

"The honor was all ours," we assured her as we said our goodbyes to everyone and headed back to prepare for the return to the United States. Our departure time was 3:30 a.m. and we were all tired, yet there was still much to do. We couldn't risk missing the flight and knowing how tired I was, I packed quickly and went to bed early. Doyle and I were ready to be back home, but I woke up feeling like there was something standing in our way. Something that did not want us to get back to the United States to tell the story of what occurred here.

As we waited in the lobby, I began to feel the pressure increasing in the atmosphere but speaking up to the others was not an option as it would only serve to set others on edge. I sat in the lobby quietly, but inside, something was stirring. Leaning over to Doyle, I whispered, "Something is wrong. I don't feel peace about this return trip."

Still Not Done

At 3:30 a.m., the cars began to arrive. The luggage was loaded, and the vehicles sat waiting as we gathered to jump in. I stood in a sleepy haze between the vehicles, watching all the activity taking place. It was just time to wait for instructions as to which car I was climb into.

Conversations were going in all directions, and I wasn't going to add to the noise with questions of my own, so I just decided to get into one of the vehicles. As I started toward the car, Doyle called my name, "Let's ride in this vehicle."

I had already gotten into the vehicle, but I had no reason to argue, so I got out and sleepily wandered over to the vehicle he chose and jumped in. Three adults in the back seat of a small Toyota, shoulder to shoulder on a trek that would last for many hours to come. It was going to be hours before we got close to civilization, so closing my eyes trying to get some sort of sleep seemed to be the logical choice.

Logical yes, but realistic no. We bounced around, bumping into each other as the driver wildly drove the windy roads full of holes at seventy miles per hour. Every now and then, we would get a glimpse of the other car we were following but not very often.

Looking at Doyle, I conveyed my feelings, "Something doesn't feel right."

"What do you think it is?" He whispered into my ear.

"Something is trying to keep this from being an easy transition," I said. He patted my hand and put his arm on the back of the seat to get some room, but also in a conveyance of supportive protection. Together, we quietly began to pray.

Dozing in and out of naps on this bumpy road, I would wake only to pray again before the next nap.

The driver continued to drive like he was in charge of a runaway roller coaster, but we were headed in the way of home, so we just relaxed into the jarring. Without fail, town after town, we were pulled over by the local Police or local Military. Four times we were pulled over and questioned. We were racing to get to the flight, as there is no room for error in time and no back up plan. Yet somehow, there was calm.

Once we got past that, it was just a short time later when we saw debris flying in front of us and a vehicle begin to flip. It was our team that was in the vehicle in front of us. I watched as their vehicle jerked violently to the right. The two left tires blew out. The vehicle then changed directions to be perpendicular to the road, clearly out of control, and abruptly came to a halt with two of the four tires lifting into the air three to four feet, putting one hundred percent of the weight of the vehicle on the already blown tires and almost flipping it into a drainage ditch.

"You have got to be kidding," flew out of my mouth. Doyle and I looked around to see if we could get out of the vehicle safely to help, but just as suddenly as the accident happened, seemingly out of nowhere, and unexplainably, the vehicle righted itself crashing back down onto all four tires. It was clear that the vehicle should have flipped with the momentum we had been traveling, but God redeemed this too. People came out of nowhere from all directions and began repairing the vehicle and before we knew it, there were new tires on the car and again we were racing down the roadway.

Doyle looked at me and spoke what I was thinking, "You know, that was the vehicle that you initially climbed into." There was nothing left to do but shake our heads at the tactics of the enemy.

We finally made it to the airport, jumped out of the vehicle and grabbed our luggage to catch up with the rest of the team.

We went through the steps of being cleared to board the flight, waited while they piled our luggage together on a huge, antiquated scale, and said goodbye to our passports, again. This was a common occurrence, which was probably the only thing on this entire trip that made me uneasy, giving my passport to someone who doesn't speak my language, being asked to move forward without it, and collect it later down the line. But my uneasiness was quickly silenced by the sudden sight of chocolate cake and Coca-Cola! Yes!! Ok look, at this point I didn't have my passport, but I had access to something that resembled home, and I was going after it. I looked at my partner, motioned to the cake and said, "I'm going in and I'm not coming back without chocolate."

I can't even lie, I know as I sat there eating my cake and drinking my coke, I probably looked way more happy and content than I should have. I was totally in the flesh and feeding every taste bud I had, but I remained unapologetic and happy. After taking a moment to indulge, we boarded a flight to Dar Es Salaam for an overnight stay. Most of the return trip was mostly normal with the occasional narrow miss of a motorcycle or someone standing in the street and refusing to move. But overall…Not too bad.

NOTE: When we got back stateside, I received an update about the woman who was hosting what I named Legion. God confirmed that I had been speaking prophetically when I explained Legion had made a covenant.

We found out through follow-ups that the woman had indeed voluntarily, albeit it in deception, made a covenant with demons for power. She made that covenant many years prior and has since refused any and all counseling or deliverance from anyone. It was the belief of the woman who hosts Legion that she would have the "best life or a better life." That included a promise to be financially secure and enjoy better health. All she needed to do was agree to make the covenant with the demons through a local witch doctor. As a result, she willingly offered the blood sacrifice of a chicken to a witch doctor in a ceremonial seal of the covenant. She has openly admitted to local Pastors that since she made the covenant, her life is no better in regards to health, finances or happiness, but to this day, she will not renounce her covenant with the dark. Her bond is deep, and her allegiance is established and remains as such.

The Next Level – The Takeaway

Prior to this mission trip, I was familiar with the demonic, encountered the demonic, and even cast out the demonic. Growing up surrounded by witches, Satanists, and psychics, I was all too familiar with how the darkness operates. However, during this trip, my comprehension further developed and personalized a completely different level of walking in faith without understanding. Proverbs 3:5 and Job 42:5. To have faith only requires trust. To understand means to have a knowledge OF but not necessarily a belief IN it.

- My choice was not of this world. My choice was not to know OF God's power but instead to TRUST IN God's power.
- My choice was not to think OF God's provision but to have FAITH IN his coverage.
- My choice was not to be OF a belief system but instead to be IN FAITH and TRUST IN testimony to come.

In other words, we can be IN the journey, or we can be OF the journey. My choice to be IN the journey of the unknown resulted in my training being increased. However, that increase occurred under conflict. As a matter of fact, my training was increased **because** of the conflict. But the Lord didn't stop there. Wisdom was optimized and multiplied under pressure. Discernment expanded under compression. Faith accelerated during opposition.

So many things in this trip changed me. As spiritually mature as I felt and as sure footed as I was before, that perspective completely changed once I experienced such a personal attack.

Like so many others, I've been attacked in my finances and in the streets of the roughest neighborhoods. I've been attacked in my spirit during my sleep. I've been attacked through my family. I've been attacked in my relationships, but this...this was sooo deeply personal. So multi-level, so calculated, so evil, so conniving to this day it's on my top ten list of things to never forget about the methodical deployment of the tools of the enemy. Isolation, deception, character assassination, physical assault, emotional manipulation, one after another. Relentlessly. I've been tested, and I am even more sure than ever. Truly rooted, strong, focused, and unmovable.

Without testing, we don't really know our own position with the Lord, and we don't know where the cracks in our armor are. We don't know how to fortify against the enemy if we do not know where our weaknesses lie. How do we have confidence in our strength if it's not tested in battle? While it may seem offensive to consider this, for me it truly is a privilege to be tested. God doesn't test us to prove anything to Him. He tests us to show us where we are in our walk with Him. To help us learn ourselves. To give us the opportunity to know our weaknesses so that we may fortify those areas into places of resilience.

This world is full of both dark and light, of evil and of goodness. How can we grow if we choose to turn a blind eye to what is all around us?

Practice, practice, practice...When God gives you the privilege of practicing before the battle, take it. That offer of practice may seem uncomfortable, scary or even unfair in some ways, but believe me, it is mercy in action. That is training in action. Do not shy away from battles because it's hard. That's like avoiding the gym and remaining immobile while trying to keep strong. It makes no sense.

There are fundament biblical truths that we must all learn to accept and even embrace.

- ✓ There is no room for fear when walking with the Lord. When we have FAITH IN knowing that we are protected and we are assured that he will provide and protect, security follows. Most of us go into battle with an empty weapon. A weapon that is designed to win, a weapon that is designed to conquer, but we don't know how to use it because we don't practice. We don't load it so that it can be ready when the ambush comes because all too often we think we will have time to load it when we need it. We don't oil it and take care of it because it takes time from our busy schedules, so when it fails, we blame the weapon. The truth is, if we take time to learn where we are in our relationship with God, we grow.
- ✓ When we take time to read the word and speak the truth of the Lord, glorifying Him in all that we do or experience, we load the weapon. It's ready when needed.
- ✓ When we step into uncomfortable times, places, or circumstances in faith, we oil our faith and create testimonies that carry forward.
- ✓ There are no formulas or equations that we can use to conjure or create a desired outcome.
- ✓ We can choose to believe in the truth, power, and majesty of Father God, or we can choose fear, worry, and anxiety issued by the Father of lies, Lucifer.

- ✓ We can participate in evil by following the direction of others, or we can join with the Spirit of God and refuse anything less than direction from Him.
- ✓ We can give attention to the enemy by using the devil as an excuse for our own open doors and our own inattentiveness to the condition of our spirit, or we can give God the glory in ALL circumstances. Searching for God's hand and knowing that the devil didn't sneak up on Him. The devil just walked through our own open doors.
- ✓ Sometimes God has to tear it down to build it up correctly. What we create, demand, who we marry, what we believe, where we are and what we have may have to be removed from us, destroyed, torn away, or be exposed in order for God to build up, provide, redirect, or correct what we thought was so good.
- ✓ Some people who say they know Jesus the man, know the teachings, believe He's their savior, and may even know all the scriptures, do not have a relationship with Him.
- ✓ The word "Christian" does not necessarily mean authority. Why? Because just wearing a cross around your neck and going to church does not build the relationship with God. That relationship takes a desire to learn about Him and an urge to follow Him. Having prayer meetings, having a ministry, praying at the table before a meal and before bed does not mean that authority is known, or understood. Christians can claim it, can say it, and can even believe it to some degree, but

if there isn't training, practice, and a consistent nurturing of that relationship, it might just be a religion. If there isn't a rooting in the relationship, there is no authority.
- ✓ Regardless of feel-good teachings, the truth is Christians can indeed be influenced by evil. And to be honest, quite often they are around us with regularity. Pride, arrogance, self-focus, lack of compassion, and a hardened heart are tools of the enemy. Ironically, a misunderstanding of what being a follower of Jesus is often leads to the very tools that the enemy uses against us. --- If Jesus didn't do it, Jesus didn't model it and if Jesus wouldn't say it, it's not Godly. Period.
- ✓ Christians can be devils in disguise. We can speak Christian lingo without our hearts being participants. Christians can speak words of encouragement then gossip when backs are turned. Christians know how to behave but if it's not in their hearts, it's empty. Saying you're a Christian does not make you part of some kind superior club that excuses devilish ways.
- ✓ The true intention of hearts will be exposed when we are surrounded by evil. Some excuse their behaviors by indicating that they are "just sensitive to the atmosphere." While this might be accurate, this is no excuse. Why? Because we are all called to be aware or "sensitive" to the spiritual atmosphere. It's biblical. But it's never an excuse for unchrist-like choices. Excuses such as they might be in a foul mood or even agitated, but sensitivity does not mean that we change our character. In truth, our character becomes unveiled and

moves into action when evil or darkened hearts become empowered by darkness. Example: Doyle was agitated by the oppressive spirits throughout our journey. HOWEVER, he never turned against me, turned away from me, never compromised me, never spoke ill of me, never minimized me, and never struck out at me verbally or in any other form. Why? Because Doyle has a loving, Christ-like character through and through. Even in total oppressive circumstances. In short, Satan plays with the toys that we give him, he doesn't create new ones.

✓ Partnering with the spiritual world creates a dis-ease and physical internal disease.
✓ There are many people who teach, preach, lead, or speak in the name of Jesus but are doing so from a hardened or darkened heart. Some of these hardened people we might want to keep close to us while knowing they are doing us wrong in order to teach them a better way. **However**, before you do, make sure that person is your **assignment** and not your self-prescribed **project**. The difference is huge. An assignment is from God. The project is from pride.
✓ There are some who will confuse forgiveness with loving from a distance. However even God has boundaries. Those who mislead, create disunity, use deception for personal gain, interrupt and drag people into places that they did not deserve to be drug into, will have their day in front of the Lord. Don't be fooled into false Christianity.

Proverbs 14:7 (NIV)

⁷ Stay away from a fool, for you will not find knowledge on their lips.

Psalm 26:4-5 (NIV)

⁴ I do not sit with the deceitful, nor do I associate with hypocrites. ⁵ I abhor the assembly of evildoers and refuse to sit with the wicked.

1 Corinthians 15:33 (NIV)

³³ Do not be misled: "Bad company corrupts good character."

- ✓ There are those who will trust behaviors and false words of repentance from another. Those who trust the empty words of those who ask for forgiveness without out the desire to be forgiven. Those who fall prey to those predators, they will be consumed by the deception. There is no reasoning with them. Move on.
- ✓ Denying forgiveness to an apology based on your own un-forgiveness is a sin in itself. – If they are truly heartsick in repentance then do not deny them the forgiveness they seek.
- ✓ Opposition in our daily lives is to be expected, but not feared. Anticipate it, but do not give it more attention than you give the Lord's hand in it. Turn your back on the temptations and refuse to give time to them.

Opposition, temptation, confusion, manipulation, and aggravation are the enemy's job. **Fire him**.
- ✓ None can understand the journey of another. Nor should we expect them to.
- ✓ The two things we can know and stand on are: the Bible and the fruit. If there's no fruit, then we must use discernment. Sometimes that means moving forward in our lives without certain people.
- ✓ If there is deception and corruption in the wake of a person or a group, it's our responsibility to ask the Lord for insight and sometimes that includes moving forward in our lives without them.
- ✓ If you are following the Lord and your focus is on what He says versus what people say, you don't need to explain yourself to anyone and you can't expect them to understand.
- ✓ Don't expect testimonies to be received by those who partner with the enemy in jealousy, envy, greed, anger, lust, selfishness, or general disregard of others. Don't expect testimonies to be received by those with spiritual immaturity, faith issues, or their unbelief.
- ✓ Those who choose to minimize God's work, actually expose the enemy working inside of them.
- ✓ Those who have become so comfortable in seeing the miracles of God become complacent in His presence. It also means we sometimes take it for granted. This is something that we should all remain aware of and work to stay out of. Exodus 40:34-38

- ✓ Sink into the spirit when those around you are responding in the flesh. Do not participate in the same entity that they are participating in. Use discernment to learn what is occurring. Ask the Lord what is going on in the spirit before determining a course of action or response.
- ✓ Those who judge you wrongly do not know you. Only the Father knows the heart. Do not be angry at those who do this. They are lost and think they are found. Let God find them and reveal to them their deceit.
- ✓ Warnings from God are not trivial or frivolous. They are heeded but not to be feared.
- ✓ Those who falsely accuse either have no discernment and are not hearing from God, or they are entertaining an agenda that speaks louder than the whisper of the Lord.
- ✓ Accusers often reveal more about themselves than they accuse of another.
- ✓ Peace beyond all understanding is often preached. However, until we experience it, it cannot be understood. Instead…speak it in terms of what can be understood so that others may benefit from your experience. Examples:
    - A calm that overtakes all chaos surrounds us.
    - A focus when there is a haze of confusion.
    - A clarity where there is a whirlwind of mess.
    - An inner knowing when in the midst of the unknown.

Doing this allows people to grab ahold of the Word with practical application and look for it in their lives.
- ✓ There's a Kingdom comfort in knowing that God knows what's pending in our individual timelines here on earth. He knows the difficulties and the joys. He knows the sorrows or suffering and He knows of the victories, but we can find rest in allowing God to do His part while we do our part of what we are purposed to do.
- ✓ Obedience is far more important than understanding. When people need all the answers before obeying, they are still leaning on their own understanding. This is a faith issue. If you are affected by someone struggling with that, please know that is their issue and not your issue to carry. That is their issue and their journey. Do not let someone else's faith issue delay your own walk with God.
- ✓ Greatest pleasures in life come from the choice and actions of yielding to God. Everything we have, will have, or have had is because God placed it there or allowed it. Our friends, family, income, talents, and gifts all come from God. When we yield to Him, we are yielding to the receiving or losing the very things He provides. Nothing belongs to us; everything is on loan. The softer we are in holding onto them the easier it is to let go.
- ✓ The path of least resistance, the most comfortable, and the most familiar are not always evidence of God. Discernment is critical because the reality is we just

- might be being lazy and making the mistake of thinking its God.
- ✓ Walking in trust and obedience of God is only as limited as we are individually. God is not limited in any way. However, we are limited. Meaning our abilities to trust and obey are only as available as we are open to being led.
- ✓ The miraculous is only as limited as we are to embrace it. A willingness to participate in our portion of assignments allows for the miraculous to occur. It's then that we get to witness it.
- ✓ Walking in faith means learning how to work within our assignments in the midst of the enemy's deterrents.

There were many things that were reinforced, I was reminded of, or I got to witness live and in person. Each one sharpened me, each one trained me up differently, and each one changed me. It was truly a blessing.

Even though throughout this trip there was a continuous collision of dark and light (some we were warned about, some we were not), God was fully in control. The enemy was active but my Father was in charge.

Somewhere along the line we have come to believe that we are to pray against the things that are uncomfortable, the things we are warned are to come, and to avoid conflict with the enemy. But why? The scriptures tell us that He will uphold us, He will guard us, He will cover us with His feathers, and we are to be strong and courageous. You can find these in Isaiah 41:10, 2 Thessalonians 3:3, Psalm 91:1-4 and Deuteronomy 31, just to name a few.

Why pray out of fear when we can stand in confidence. We can believe the promises that He will be our covering, our protection, and our deliverer from evil if we are in relationship with Him.

God doesn't run around trying to keep up with the fiendish doings of the Devil. Satan doesn't get the privilege of tricking God. Satan is beneath God and subject to God's manipulation. The book of Job confirms that God used Job to mess with the Devil. The Devil wasn't outsmarting God.

If God is God, then it's my job to let Him be who He is to be, and I am to be who I am created to be. I am to follow, and He is to lead. There really isn't any other option other than rebellion.

God loved me enough to warn me and I love Him enough to trust Him. I went knowing that I was walking into something that only He could protect me from. He allowed me to be in a position where I knew no one and I had no leverage or familiar ground to retreat to. He permitted me to be in a position in which I could do battle on my own based on what I knew, or to be humble and lean on Him. The timing was impeccable as I was physically incapable of any physical combat with her because my shoulder was incapable. In other words, the Lord took away all the tools that I was familiar with, and I was blessed and redeemed.

I received the privilege of witnessing and living out Proverbs 3:5-6 (CSB).

"Trust in the Lord with all your heart, and do not rely on your own understanding; in all your ways know him, and he will make your paths straight"

We must remember that God is the ultimate power. Nothing that exists anywhere, occurs without God's knowledge or permission. So why would I need to pray against something that God has permitted? I know what it means to be prayed up now. I know what it is to be prepared for combat of any sort. I know what it is to be used in a totally different way and I'm ready with my "yes and amen."

He was showing me something at a greater level. He raised the stakes, took me off the bench, and invited me into the game. Just like in sports, in order to make the goal, there will be plenty of contact from the opposing team, but if you want to make that goal, you choose to get up off the bench. He was using me for something! That is exciting, why would I get in the way of that?

He showed me a sample of the magnitude of the power He provides. He showed me that regardless of who tries to attack my character, I don't have to fight back, my Father fights my battles. When my body was physically weak, my strength came from Him. In other words, in many ways, I got the privilege of living out 2 Corinthians 12:10 (CSB).

"So I take pleasure in weaknesses, insults, hardships, persecutions, and in difficulties, for the sake of Christ. For when I am weak, then I am strong."

He showed me that even at my weakest I was my strongest. He showed me His love for those who are lost and seeking. He showed me how far He will go to display who He is. He showed people that He's present now and not a story from long ago. He showed me that some people will compromise their own character to hang onto what is familiar. He showed me that sometimes He will go to great lengths to expose the enemy, while other times He will just let the enemy's arrogance and pride reveal their identity.

So much was set into motion, why would anyone want to interfere in that? God protected, empowered, covered, sustained, provided, and loved me all the way through it. Ambushes had no power. Fights had no power. Assaults had no power. Accidents had no power. Time restraints had no power. Character assassination attempts had no power. Anger had no power. God's power was the only power which remained.

When we are caught in conflict, we must be willing to listen to the direction of the Lord. Often, all He wants is us to stay humble so he can do His job.

The truth is Satan is actually quite boring, but he is a definite overachiever. If you know that he likes to break down people, a system, unity, family, and trust, then you take away his power. If you see the desperation to derail us on our mission in Satan's plans, then ask yourself why. It just might be that we are succeeding in glorifying God and that just might be angering the enemy. If you choose to see the anxiety of Satan as he loses his grip on those that he's ruled with fear or domination, then you can smile at the understanding that Satan fears you and Satan fears me.

The reality is Satan is unoriginal, unimaginably handicapped, and not omnipresent. He's restricted in who, what, and where he's influencing, and he is not unilaterally operating in any real authority. Satan, Lucifer, the Devil, however he is referenced, needs two things to operate.

- Approval

- And his army

You see…

- Satan is limited to time, space, approval, and participation.
- Don't give him credit for what God may be allowing.
- Don't waste time worrying about the enemy, just pay attention and stay aware.
- Take notice as to what you believe. You might just be more in agreement with the enemy than you are in God's promise, provision, or coverage.
- Don't give over your authority to the enemy just because he convinces you that you don't have it to start with.

Conclusion

Step by step

Learn His Presence

Learn how to discern God's voice in your spirit from the voice of the enemy. This can be done and is done with practice and while building a relationship in God and in the Word.

Humility

Choose obedience and submission to the Will of the Father. Not out of fear but out of Love for Him. A Trust in His perfect plan. A Faith that He will work all things for His good and the good of the Kingdom of God. An understanding that when we make ourselves smaller and selfless, God becomes bigger in our lives, and we see things differently.

Stay Within YOUR Assignments

Know what you are called to do and do it. Not what people tell you what you are called to do. If you don't know, sit, seek, knock, enter, and listen. Patience is critical in knowing your assignments. The enemy will always tempt us to follow his lead when the Father wants us to follow His lead.

Be Spirit Led

No matter what something looks like, or feels like in the flesh, we must go to God first and listen to the truth over any circumstance. We are surrounded by lies of the enemy at all times. This doesn't make the enemy powerful. It just makes him consistent. We must be just as consistent in listening to the truth of God. Going only where He says to go, when He says to do it.

Being spirit led means that we are letting the Lord define who we are and what He wants for us each and every day. The darkness loves to watch us squirm. So, recognize the games of the enemy for what they are, games. Don't get angry. Anger derails us.

Manipulation of Mission

No matter how many Jezebels, or how many Legions, or how many ailments or derailments seem to be standing in the way, God sees the bigger picture.

It's our responsibility to recall the truths God had spoken to us, through us, or over us in our lifetime. Regardless of our age or stage of life, God gave each of us promises. As a child perhaps. Or maybe when something was occurring in your life that made you feel lost or forgotten. Whatever it is and whenever it was, God gave you a gift, a direction, a promise, a sense of who you truly are. God never leaves anything unfinished. Ask Him about that gift, ask Him about those promises. Ask Him how you got off track and how to get back on. Think about the promise God gave you. Ask Him to remind you again.

He is with us forever, never detaching Himself. He's always talking. He's always reaching for us and waiting for us to reach back to remember Him.

Let Him Pave the Way

Regardless of what's thrown at us, the level of darkness that shows up, the way things appear throughout our journey or our life, God's plan prevails. He paves the way in each of our lives.

P. Frederick

He did not create us to flounder and feel lost. He created us to stay connected and commune with Him. To pray within His will and all will be done. To know we are loved and to love others. To know our authority and wield it wisely. To rest under Him when it's time to rest.

From the warning dreams to personal attacks…from cultural divides to physical attacks…God had a plan. Don't get stuck and marred in the detail or the emotion.

God is In Charge. Remember…as He spoke to me many times and as I have written before, "The beginning of <u>all things</u> is written. The end of <u>all things</u> is written. We just have to live through the pages in between." It's already done.

Selah

www.ingramcontent.com/pod-product-compliance
Lightning Source LLC
Chambersburg PA
CBHW061725070526
44583CB00024B/3006